ENGLISH VILLAGERS

LIFE IN THE COUNTRYSIDE

ENGLISH VILLAGERS
LIFE IN THE COUNTRYSIDE

VALERIE PORTER

Bounty
Books

500994 553

First published in 1992 by George Philip Limited

This edition published 2004 by Bounty Books,
a division of Octopus Publishing Group Limited,
2-4 Heron Quays, London E14 4JP

A CIP catalogue record for this book is available
from the British Library

ISBN 0 7537 0892 2

Design Vivienne Brar
Page design Kathy Gummer
Typeset by Keyspools Limited

Printed and bound in China

Contents

Introduction

〜〜〜

The English villager is fading away. However hard we try to preserve the fabric of the village, or perhaps because we do so, we have almost lost sight of the real villager in a rosy haze of nostalgia. By pretending to be villagers ourselves, importing urban attitudes and fossilizing a dream of village life that has little to do with reality, we have effectively destroyed the living context we seek to occupy. Nearly all of us are tourists now, aware of a lost dream but not of the reality of that dream.

Very few of those who live in villages today are villagers in the true sense of those whose working and social lives are inextricably bound up with the village; very few appreciate the vital, age-old relationship between the village and its working countryside – a relationship that was the reason for the community's existence. In our own century we have finally broken the village's umbilical tie to the land that gave it birth, roots and reality.

In the past, the village had certain characteristics that identified it as a self-contained community set within its own geographical and social boundaries, fending for itself, supplying virtually all its own day-to-day needs from cradle to grave and rarely bothering to look outwards. It was small, typically having a population of perhaps 200, and to some degree inevitably inbred. The village was an extended family, with its own bounded social hierarchy.

Families can be both needed and resented by those unable to escape from them, and the village could be a prison as well as a haven. When the economic ties that were even more binding than kinship became dissipated during the 19th century, the strength of village self-sufficiency and family spirit declined, while the demands of the individual increased: the rebellious child, seeking adolescent independence from its village parent, was offered the means to leave home and to cut those formidable apron-strings. In the 20th century, the individual villager has fully achieved liberation but, ironically, the townsman now seeks to return to the reassuringly small community that the villager had escaped.

The structure of village life has completely altered and many villages have been almost overwhelmed by the unprecedented speed of change that has occurred during the last century or so. These changes are reflected in the fabric of the village in the encroachment of blocks of non-vernacular buildings and the rapid disappearance of essential local services, so that the village has lost its heart

OPPOSITE **An annual street picnic in Northcott Mouth, Cornwall, at the turn of the century. The tables, chairs and hot water were provided, but the villagers brought their own food.**

and become but a shell invaded by settlers from the towns. The latter might yet succeed in revitalizing the villages but only as outlying fragments of the suburbs that now blanket this small country in spirit, if not yet physically.

The village today is virtually the antithesis of its own tradition: it is no longer self-sufficient and instead generally depends on the town for goods, services, employment, culture and the maintenance of its infrastructure. Having lost control of its own affairs, the countryside has become the town's toy, an unreal and quaint place serving as a romantic backdrop to the stage of urban life. Sadly, in the eyes of the majority, the countryside and its villages are no longer permitted the dignity of being the real stage where people work and have their being.

The tale of villagers in recent generations is one of separation and divorce between employers and employed, between rural rich and poor, and above all between town and country. The crucial period for the development of these polarizations was during the reign of Queen Victoria. This book concentrates on the period from about 1850 to 1939, a time which remains in the oral tradition of older villagers born before World War I, who in their youth experienced a different village to that of today but even then not the all-embracing, working rural village which forms the heart of this book.

The Victorian decades also saw the birth of photography. For the first time in history, the image of the village and its people became permanently captured on paper: freeze-frames that caught a moment in the moving picture of village life. These two-dimensional images recorded by the camera can only be brought to life by the memories of older villagers. The picture they reveal can be just as enriching as the romance; and those who understand the reality of the past are much better able to live the present and stimulate the future. This must be to the benefit of the village itself as a living, vibrant community – and it is in the interests of the survival of the real and busy village that this book has been written. I have great faith in the ability of the village to fight back by adapting, and to live and thrive.

Or am I too optimistic? Even in my own lifetime, villages and their villagers have changed. Although it is always a risk to revisit golden memories, I recently returned to my childhood village in rural Wiltshire. I went with a longing tinged with fear that I would not recognize it and would feel lost in an alien place with no familiar landmarks, a stranger wandering through my own memory. I was still a child when I finally left Wiltshire in 1950 and had not been back since.

As it happens, the village near my childhood home was where photography was born in 1838 and quietly nursed by its parent, William Henry Fox Talbot, whose family had lived for several centuries in a magnificent riverside abbey beside Lacock, a village which has been preserved almost intact, frozen in time, by the National Trust.

As I approached Wiltshire, I flicked through the pages of my childhood memory at random, gleaning an image of the old stone horse-trough regularly visited by cart-horses; the iron village pump with a squeak (no one had mains water or electricity then); the tight stone cottages jostling with no daylight between their shoulders, as if they were but a single haphazard building lining the street; damp watermeadows and the old stone bridge with its several arches under which a child could squeeze through by the river and keep dry-footed – just – to watch the kingfishers and minnows; the 13th-century abbey discreet behind its heavy ivy curtains, and the dusty little lane along which I had so often wandered home, daydreaming, or been carried on the back of an adult's bicycle. Cars were rare in rural areas then.

OPPOSITE **A 1920s film crew records rural life in the Sussex village of Amberley.**

8

Now it was October 1990. My heart sinking rapidly, I tried to ignore the tourist signposts pointing to Lacock. In my childhood the village felt as if it was still protected by the old family, though books tell me it was handed to the Trust in 1944. I shuddered at the sight of a Trust caravan, selling mementoes no doubt, parked hard by the abbey's magnificent iron gates. The abbey itself, glimpsed in the distance, was so much cleaner and more exposed than I remembered: its wall creepers had been removed and it seemed to have been scrubbed, rejuvenated, and to have lost some of the magic of its antiquity. It did not look its age and, like a film-star after a face-lift, it had lost some of its character and become self-conscious.

The watermeadows had been drained and the river was more like a stream: it, too, had been taken in hand, cleaned up and 'improved'. How I missed its ramshackle rushes and reeds, and the slippery green stones under the arches!

I wandered into the village. It was perfectly preserved – and quite dead. It was a village on show, a village for passing strangers, not a village for living in and gossiping in. An old man tended his garden by one of the many little stone bridges over the upper reaches of the stream; he paused to chat to some tourists but, though his accent was genuine, his words had a well-rehearsed tone to them as if his remarks and phrases were prepared for the tourists who come to Lacock in their thousands to gaze at its frozen Englishness: eternal outsiders seeking the heart of a village which no longer seems to have one.

I wandered disconsolately through the square of streets and up one or two tiny back lanes, noticing how the buildings had been so carefully maintained with no external modern touches to ruin the period feel. It *looked* like an old village but to me, the adult, it was no longer alive as it had been to the child. There were no villagers loitering in the street, no children, no noise, no work, no smells, no untidiness, no gossip except from the high buzz of a thousand bees and hoverflies gorging on the pollen of the ivy that demurely covered every sheltered, sun-kissed old stone wall of the bridges and gardens.

Lacock was no longer my childhood village, however enchanting it looked. It was a film-maker's set, a ghost village even when thronged with onlookers. No doubt the villagers exist, emerging furtively at dusk after the tourists have gone, but where was the everyday life of the village? For a village is, essentially, its inhabitants, not its buildings, though the guide-books tend to describe buildings rather than the everyday people who keep a village warm.

Warily, I drove a few miles down the road to another, smaller stone village from my childhood. It, too, was far quieter than it had been. I missed the village idiot grinning by the wall, who used to be mocked, but kindly, and for whom there was considerable and protective affection. I missed the sound of children in the playground of our one-room school which now seemed to be a storage place. I sorely missed the old sweet-shop with its bell-tinking door and multicoloured jars of delights: it was now a private house. I missed the wells that had stood in so many front gardens, all now safely covered over since the village had attached itself to the mains water supply. I missed the burble of gossiping women at their gates and the knots of men chatting, remembering, guffawing, smoking and passing the time of day as men still do in Mediterranean villages, and the ubiquitous cluckity chickens and the ducks that snoozed in the street, napping between bursts of animated duck-chat. I could not imagine that today's villagers would still bowl for live pigs and geese at the local fête, as we had done.

The village had, for the most part, escaped the attentions of incomers, though the street's cottages were no doubt commuter homes. The old sawmill was even now in the process of being developed into expensive houses: the first stage of the village's demise was under way. But apart from the handful of council houses that had been there even 40 years ago, there was very little new building and no 1930s bungalows and villas or 1960s commuter estates.

It is not necessarily good that a village should not grow; nor, conversely, is it necessarily good that it *should* grow. Perhaps the problem now is that growth is imposed from outside, rather than from within the village, developing to meet its own needs at its own pace. Lacock is frozen, and alien to the returning child – it is a place of preserved buildings rather than homes and workplaces for villagers – and even my 'secret' village, like so many others, has become a ghost village during the day.

Pondering, I returned to my present home, a very small farm cottage in a valley of hamlets scattered around a growing Sussex village where I have been parish clerk for several years and have learned much about the nuts, bolts and heart of village life.

Within living memory this village was no more than a few handfuls of sandstone cottages and farms. It is now thriving in its own way but only by having changed quite radically, especially within the last 30 years in which it has

The shape of things to come: new council houses in the 1920s.

embraced, unwillingly at times, a rash of new homes built, not for indigenous village families whose surnames can be deciphered on tombstones at least a century or two old, but for people who have migrated from cities and suburbs in search of a better life in 'the country' – country with which they have long since lost touch and whose realities they often fail to understand. They are people of today who have lost the context of yesterday and are unwittingly the poorer for that loss. Many of them are itinerants who pause here awhile but move on under the demands of their employment, restless nomads forever in search of greener pastures, opportunists in true nomad fashion, staying long enough perhaps to operate, in all innocence, the equivalent of a slash-and-burn policy, taking their fill of what they see as village life but without the commitment to let the village's interests dominate their own. Having tasted, and become disenchanted or bored, they move on, rootless, leaving the original villagers bereft of services the old depended upon but which lapsed because these mobile, affluent newcomers had not required them.

I have lived in rural areas for most of my life and have over the years listened to many elderly people who have spent all their lives in villages. As parish clerk to the village in which I now live, I have had the privilege of coming to know every villager, whether original or newcomer, and have heard about their problems and hopes and listened to their complaints and their opinions. I have seen, through their eyes as well as my own and those of other parish clerks all over the country, how village life has changed – is still changing – and in particular how the main breadwinner in most families now rarely works in or even near the village itself. And that, perhaps, is the key to the new village and its present loss of identity: people now only play at being villagers and rarely work within it, or for it, so that the place is empty and silent by day. Dead. What happened to all those villagers who once gave the village so much life?

Part 1
The Living Village

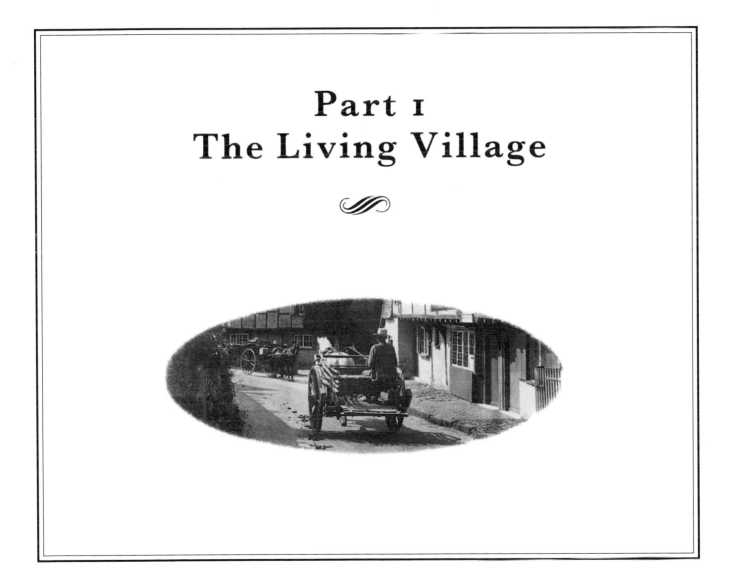

CHAPTER I

Bones

Consider, first, the village as it is now, and then search for the new village at its heart. What was daily village life like when Victoria was still a young queen? How did the village change during her reign, and in what ways does it differ now? These are some of the questions this book seeks to answer.

Perhaps the first question should be, 'What is a village?' There is no measurement, no magic number of buildings or acres or inhabitants that defines the difference between village and town: it is more a state of mind, a social and emotional concept rather than a physical one. Villages are what people make of them and they are, essentially, communities of villagers – living organisms, not static groups of cottages and public buildings set in unchanging landscapes. Villages need people.

And a village is more than its centre. There are numerous homes and holdings dotted about the area which consider themselves to be part of the village and depend upon it as their nearest economic and social centre. They form the village's hinterland, though they might be so sparsely scattered that only the locals recognize the affinity. Some are separate manors or farms; some are isolated cabins and cottages; some gather to form little hamlets, like moons orbiting the planet village. The spirit of belonging counts more than the physical distribution of the houses.

The village's character has in most cases been determined by gradual accretion over many lifetimes and has been influenced by individual villagers as much as by the mightier forces of aristocracy, land-ownership and government. Its physical structure is the framework for the flesh of village society and it reflects the changing patterns of village life during its history: it is the persisting evidence of the existence of villagers and, long after individuals have died even in memory, their conversations and emotions linger in the buildings they once inhabited and in the streets and greens where they bustled and strolled.

Villages come in infinite variety but tend to be complementary to the landscape. Shorn of 20th-century additions, most villages fit comfortably into their environment, because most of them have always been a part of the land itself. They seem to grow out of it and, within it, to

PREVIOUS PAGE **Traffic 'thundering' through the quiet village of Byworth in Sussex.**

embrace themselves and their inhabitants. Describing Devonshire's widespread use of cob early in the 19th century, Charles Vancouver said that it was 'utterly impossible, at a distance, to distinguish a village from a beatfield, both having uniformly the same shade; and from both of which the stranger perceives smoke issuing.'

Remember the land and look at it with clear eyes. Wherever the village, and whatever its role today, almost invariably it was originally gripped tightly by the land. In 1850 half the population of England lived in rural areas and nearly everyone in the village worked directly or indirectly with the land. Every individual was acutely aware of seasons, cycles, weather, crop disasters, cattle plagues, of nature at its most wilful and powerful, helping or hindering the harvest of grain, flesh and fibre. It was agriculture that shaped most of the English landscape, many of our villages and most of our society. At the dawn of the 19th century, agriculture dominated the national economy and it is as well to remember this essential bond with the land and landscape, even today – or perhaps especially today when so many have become divorced from the reality of the working countryside. For a village to live, it needs to work, and to understand fully the development of the village it is essential to appreciate its relationship to the land.

The shape of the old village can betray something of its social history. Some villages are delineated by the parkland boundaries of the local landowner, who probably owned most of the village and carefully controlled its development in the past – more firmly and successfully than any local council planning officer. Some huddle cosily

LEFT **Runswick in North Yorkshire seems almost to have been hewn from the cliffs. Still a very active fishing village when this photograph was taken by Frank Meadow Sutcliffe (born in 1853), it was also a centre for jet-mining, one of Yorkshire's oldest industries.**

Children playing on the village green, c. 1904.

in accordance with local needs and local topography. Infinite variety is (or was) the key to the English countryside, in its scenery, its climate, its work, its farming, its customs, its buildings and its inhabitants. There are no 'typical' villages or villagers.

About ten per cent of English villages have greens and a third of them are in the seven counties that more or less formed the old kingdom of Essex, clustering around London. Very often the main role of the green was as a communal meeting-place. It was the setting for visiting entertainers and preachers; the stage for village dancing and singing, for bargaining or chatting or lounging; the place for mocking miscreants as they sat sullenly in the embarrassing embrace of the stocks. It was often the site, too, of the communal water source and the tall wooden maypole, and probably a substantial tree – perhaps an old marriage oak or a market tree in lieu of a more formal village cross marking a gathering point for buying and selling. In times gone by the village green would have been full of life; now it is emptier and quieter, a little forlorn and aimless, too often a contrived playground with no genuine role and no robust meaning in the everyday life of the village. The actors have deserted their stage.

around a central feature; some line up neatly along a street; some have developed more stragglingly along a road or the line of a stream, as if hesitating on the way to somewhere else and just resting a while on the journey. Some villages have evolved around and comfortably enfold a road junction, dwindling away along the various lanes that curve lazily as they leave the village. Some seem to have spread at random, without much cohesion; some were clearly planned as complete units by 18th- and 19th-century landowners setting their footprints in the history of the landscape. Some are amalgamations – little islands linked together over the years as they have grown towards each other; some have clearly wandered in the course of time, their centre of gravity shifting in response to new attractions.

There is no such thing as a typical village. Most villages, except the 'all-at-once' models, developed simply

The street and back lanes form the skeleton of the village. Along them the buildings jostle, often shoulder to shoulder – cottages, houses, pubs and shops, in a pleasantly jumbled terrace of varied rooflines, jutting frontages of assorted

on a level with the parson. Writing in 1936, Sydney R. Jones described the inhabitants of such houses as 'men of refinement given to study, adventurers anchored after long travels, and tradesmen with gold in their pockets ... seeking for peace in the countryside.' Many a successful Victorian built a 'country house' in or near the village and in due course these minor mansions became the homes of retired brigadiers and naval captains, or doctors, professors, wealthy widows, redundant squires, well-off town-dwellers seeking rural bolt-holes, or the fading remnants of landed families ravaged by death duties and taxes.

Some of the larger farmhouses are as imposing as these smaller 'manor houses', and indeed some were originally genuine manor houses. The agricultural revival of the 18th century was reflected in the enlarging of farmhouses and the building of new ones on the village outskirts. In contrast, in bad times even old manor houses might suffer

LEFT **A village street, c. 1890, which shows a good mixture of building materials including cob, flint, brick, board, clay tiles and thatch.**

BELOW **Joseph Neeld began rebuilding this fine Wiltshire manor house in 1848 – the work was still incomplete when he died in 1856.**

materials and ages, harmonious in their individuality. It is the ingenious and ingenuous variety that creates and gives life to the whole.

Usually the most conspicuous buildings are the church and the 'big house'. These two institutions, representing the twin dominance of parson and squire in village life, are also very often the oldest structures. They represent a sense of continuity in the village, solid presences which remind individuals that human life is transient but that the village as an organism outlives them just as it preceded them.

The big house, maybe a manor house situated close to the church, naturally attracted the best local builders who constantly embellished and reformed it according to fashionable ideas imported from far beyond the narrow world of the village itself. Most villages have one or two other houses of substance, originally the homes of, say, estate stewards or merchants, a social stratum more or less

the indignity of being used as grainbins, implement stores and cowbyres: you can sometimes detect the tidemark of manure on manorial walls.

Other notable buildings include the mill, the village inn, and perhaps almshouses built at the instigation of a local benefactor who probably also built the old village school. Many schools, however, were simply the front room of a dwelling, while old workshops were often either part of the home, or a lean-to in the cottage yard.

The 18th and 19th centuries saw the building of some rather stark red-brick chapels by village Nonconformists. At first, bricks had plenty of local character, whatever the

A horse working a pugmill to prepare clay at the South Cove brickworks of B.A. Rous & Son, Wrentham, Suffolk.

building. On the claylands they were handmade close to the actual building site, in a village or estate brickworks, using the local clay, and there was very little uniformity of colour, size or quality. In Wiltshire, for example, where the traditional building materials were stone, chalk pug and flint, brick at first crept gently into the villages in a yellowish-white colour that blended with the older buildings. In 1841 the 'awful visitation' of major flooding demolished many of the old chalk-pug cottages in Shrewton and neighbouring villages, and they were rebuilt in the mellow local brick with the help of generous public funding.

The Victorians loved brick and, with the abolition of the brick tax in 1850, brick sizes became standardized and mass-produced rather than handmade. Huge quantities of bricks were transported by rail all over the country with the result that local bricks became more expensive than mass-produced ones, the widespread distribution of which brought uniformity over large areas instead of bricks which everybody could recognize as being from such-and-such a brickfield. Wiltshire, like other counties, found itself blighted by jarring red bricks of a much harsher colour than the ones produced from local kilns.

Above all, and predominantly, the village consists of residential buildings, and the real social history of the village is revealed by its cottages, though their stories are rarely recorded like those of the more self-important houses. Early cottages, roughly built of wattle-and-daub or timber, did not last long but were constantly rebuilt. In truth, most of the older cottages that remain today are misnamed: they were not usually the homes of labourers but of those higher up the social ladder – tradesmen, craftsmen and small farmers who could afford to build something more substantial than the typical mud hovel that was a real cottager's dwelling.

Until recently, each village evolved its own local style of cottage architecture, threading it through generations, relying on local materials, owing nothing to architectural drawings but everything to a long tradition of local builders who knew their craft, knew their materials, knew which techniques had stood the test of time in local conditions and, above all, knew their own villages and villagers. Under the eye of the squire, they perpetuated the local feel so that the villagescape remained cohesive and 'felt right'. Truly they had a sense of place.

Later, builders and their clients became more strongly influenced by broader fashions so that the same type of building occurred in villages many miles apart. The vernacular architecture of the old village began to succumb to Victorian ideas of 'progress' – that is, to the styles of the towns. As the old landed families lost influence in the village, the feeling of continuity in the landscape was broken and urban styles were stamped at random on rural communities.

During the 20th century the village and the countryside began to accommodate new features, characterized by their hardness, straightness and bulk. White-lined roads with tarmac surfaces, lines of telegraph poles and massively marching electricity pylons were rigidly imposed upon natural contours, traditional boundaries and winding, wandering lanes. From the 1890s onwards there was the intrusion of blocks of new buildings in the shape of council housing estates, roadside ribbons of inter-war bungalows and commuter estates as townsfolk began to return to the villages, bringing with them their urban ways. These newcomers arrived as conquerors and increasingly as buyers, resulting in yet another major change in village life. In Victorian times about 90 per cent of homes in Britain were rented: today the situation is quite the reverse with two-thirds of all homes owner-occupied.

CHAPTER 2

The Early Victorian Village

Traditionally, the social structure of the village was tied to the land and, despite changes during the 18th and early 19th centuries, this was still the situation in the early Victorian village of 1850. While some of the certainties of the past were being challenged, most villagers knew their own status and worth within their small community. Contributing to the general welfare of the village, each person was expected to carry out their allotted role, both economically and socially.

The aristocracy and the Church had dominated rural life for a very long time, but the relationship between these two groups was not constant: though often hand-in-glove with the governing class, the Church sometimes found itself at war with the lords of the land. The family of the local lord or squire possessed the greatest standing and wealth and thus also carried the greatest responsibility for the villagers' welfare. Almost as highly regarded in terms of social standing was the parson, backed by the power of the Church.

On a social level below the squire, and often aspiring to climb up beside him, were the farmers, consisting of the remaining handful of substantial yeoman farmers who still owned their land, and the larger group of tenant farmers who rented land from the main estate. Many farmers played an active role in local affairs and some employed 'husbandmen' (the old term for agricultural workers), though in 1850 most farmworkers were employed on the estate. Indeed, nearly everyone in the village worked on the estate, directly or indirectly, either on the home farm or on tenanted farms, in the fields and woodlands, in the dairy, or in the big house itself as domestic servants, grooms, coachmen, gardeners and the like. This helped preserve the sense of a single community within and for which people at all levels worked as well as lived. It was a secure world in which everyone contributed to the local economy.

In the social pyramid below the squire, the parson and the farmers were the village worthies, including a wide range of traders and craftworkers, who fulfilled almost all the community's needs. Most of this group worked their own smallholdings, raising a few cattle and the ubiquitous backyard pigs and poultry. Many also filled various posts within the village such as constable or clerk or served on one of the endless independent functional bodies and boards in charge of this and that at a local level – paupers, roads, schooling, drains, burials and general welfare.

OPPOSITE **Three generations of a cottage-garden family. Cottagers have been famous flower-growers since a colony of Flemish weavers held flower festivals in Norwich in the 1630s.**

RIGHT **Almshouse residents in Bridport, Dorset, in 1915. Almshouses offered free residences with free food and fuel. In return, residents obeyed certain rules, such as being good neighbours with each other.**

Those who formed the broad base of this social pyramid were hired landworkers, smallholders and other cottagers. Many followed a trade as a sideline, undertaking specialist roles such as village pig-killer or rat-catcher, or pursuing a minor craft in the village or woods, or maintaining a cottage industry which, far from being a hobby, contributed substantially and vitally to the household's income and often involved the whole family. Diversity of employment was a feature of village life at all levels, of necessity as much as by habit or choice.

The population in many counties was increasing faster than people were able to support themselves and the level of rural poverty remained high for much of the 19th century; the average family size was large and the cottages were small, rudimentary and crowded.

The urge to serve the village was strong throughout the Victorian period. George Dew (1846–1928) was typical of his age. The son of a local builder in the Oxfordshire village of Lower Heyford, Dew was appointed Relieving Officer for the Bletchington district of the Bicester Poor Law Union, a post he retained from 1870 to 1923. He also served as rate collector, inspector of nuisances, vaccination officer, school attendance officer, parish clerk and churchwarden – as well as continuing to help in the family building and carpentry trade. Travelling widely by foot, by pony, by bicycle and in due course by motor car, Dew was responsible for some 20 villages and hamlets. His father was also a man of many parts: builder, printer, newsagent and census enumerator. George's wife, Mary, known as Polly, was headmistress of the village school for nearly half a century.

Much of Dew's work concerned the poor of his region and his diaries show that poverty, which bound the villager to the village, remained a powerful bond well into the 20th century. Poverty was the familiar, if unwelcome, companion of most villagers and had always been one of the major factors in village life – grinding, unmitigated, endless, soul-destroying poverty. As his diaries reveal, Dew was often incensed by the illiberal attitudes to the poor shown by some members of his own Board of Guardians, especially farmers and clergymen, but was particularly impressed by the character of a gypsy woman, Susannah 'Sookey' Smith. Tall and well-built, with a dark, swarthy complexion, Sookey never married though she lived with various men and bore their children, including a daughter Sophia 'born by the hedge-side on a cock of hay on the old

Roman Akeman Street', and a son Ernest Merry whose father was a miller. Sookey told Dew many tales of her life as a traveller and the pleasure of camping on Cottisford Heath 'in the palmy days of old when no policeman disturbed their repose, nor hindered them in their wanderings'. But like many gypsies of the time, Sookey became a house-dweller and received parochial relief – a mere half-a-crown a week – for many years until she developed cancer of the tongue which literally starved her to death at the age of 74.

The care of the poor had for centuries been left to the Church and to private charity until the Elizabethan Poor Law encouraged the village to look after its own paupers. However, a major source of care for the disadvantaged continued to be based on personal charity – with strings attached. Lord Egremont was typical of his class in distributing a bounty of clothes made of strongest Yorkshire cloth – but only to recipients who had been certified as 'sober and industrious' by respectable householders in their own parish. Egremont also distributed soup (made from barrelled beef, Scotch barley and potatoes) three or four times a week and gave, in true squirely fashion, beef and pork pies to as many as 400 families at Christmas. At his home, Petworth House, Egremont retained a surgeon-apothecary for the express purpose of attending the poor, *gratis*, and secured the training of a woman at the British Lying-In Hospital to act as midwife, and another to inoculate the poor against various diseases. Fortunate was the villager who happened to come under the care of such a benevolent lord of the manor!

Wealthy individuals had always relieved their consciences by helping the local poor, albeit often so patronizingly that their caring was regarded with deep suspicion or as an insult. Apart from the lady of the manor's gift-bearing visits to poor cottagers, there were some more lasting, concrete gestures – or, rather, edifices of brick and stone – in the form of almshouses built by private benefactors as charitable alternatives to the appalling workhouses. There were also many other, smaller village charities founded for the benefit of the poor or elderly or widowed or whatever other cause took the benefactor's fancy, and they illustrate that strong sense of obligation which the more caring (or heaven-seeking) well-off families felt towards their own villagers. In the village of 1850, these gifts of clothes, annual bags of flour and coal or few pence were of real value to the recipients.

In a life of relentless hard work, which bound the villagers together in one way, shared social activities were equally important in cementing the community. There was little artificial division between work and play: both were part of the life of the village and took place largely within it. Entertainments – to lift people's hearts a little, if not necessarily their minds or souls – were generated by the villagers themselves, providing a rich mixture of activities to fill such brief leisure hours as there might be. The simplest was the traditional Sunday evening stroll down the village street, after church or chapel, to see and be seen, to pass the time of day, to make your face familiar and to remind other villagers of your existence.

It was vital to be able to look forward to familiar calendar breaks – the high days and holidays that broke the monotony and marked the passing of the year. Calendar festivals were still being celebrated with considerable merrymaking, each with their specific customs which often varied from village to village. The ancient rural festivals had direct relevance to everyday village life: they were closely connected with the seasonal rhythms of nature and farming. They marked midsummer, midwinter, the solstices and equinoxes, or the start or completion of specific farming activities such as ploughing,

haymaking, the corn harvest or sheep-shearing, or the fairs at which produce and livestock were sold. They were frequently centred on fertility rites, in varying degrees of explicitness: fertility, be it of soil, livestock or humans, was an important reality in the life of the countryside, and the rituals, while hugely enjoyable, had a serious undercurrent in that crop failures would directly affect every man, woman and child in the village. Initially based on superstition, the rituals gave a good excuse for expressing the pagan spirit and having fun – behaving wildly, eating and drinking and singing and dancing and shouting and no doubt conceiving a new generation. All these activities were shared with an unavoidably close-knit, familiar and virtually tribal group of largely interrelated people: the inescapable village.

Like the Puritans, Victorian moralists frowned on traditional festivities as unhealthy gatherings bound to end in riots, intemperance and every conceivable vice. To remedy this they gradually turned the remaining village celebrations into temperate, well-scrubbed, family affairs. Traditional events were either brought into the church, beaten into submission, or simply replaced by new 'traditions'. By 1850 village celebrations had become dull and respectable compared to the gloriously bawdy and vulgar events of previous years.

The simple matter of scouring the white horses of the chalk hills illustrates the change nicely. On Queen Victoria's accession in 1837, Tom Hughes recorded that the ancient White Horse carved into the chalk hillside at Uffington, Oxfordshire, had been scoured during a 'pastime' with plenty of games and entertainments to encourage the serious business of cleaning up the horse's outline. There was 'climmin' a greasy pole for a leg of mutton'; there were races for a live pig and a cheese, donkey races for a flitch of bacon, men cracking each other's heads and cudgel-playing for a gold-laced hat and a pair of buckskin breeches. John Morse of Uffington 'grinned agin another chap droo hos collars, a fine bit of spwoart, to be sure, and made the folks laaf'. But the last 'pastime' was in 1857, and Arthur Gibbs of Gloucestershire noted that nobody thought to scour the horses for the Queen's Diamond Jubilee in 1897. As the ballad went: 'The ould White Horse wants zettin' to rights'. But its magic had been lost during Victoria's reign and nobody cared much any more.

May Day, the celebration of the birth of summer, had already been deprived of much of its earlier bawdiness. No more vanishing into the woods on the eve of May Day when all the village's young and not-so-young indulged in a night of extramarital and premarital dalliance; no more bringing home the branches and flowers that symbolized fertility. By the 1870s May Day had become merely a children's day. Referring to it in his diaries, George Dew noted that the children 'dressed in every gay colour possible, with all the fine pieces of coloured ribands for adornment they could obtain' and marched around the village singing and carrying their May garlands, including 'a good number of flags and two Union Jacks among them', collecting as much money as possible for a tea at the school in the afternoon. 'Some of the poor women were up nearly all night,' commented Dew, 'in washing and getting up their white frocks in the best style; and the clean, nay some of them spotlessly pure, appearance they had spoke well for the general character of the Heyford poor.'

Other festivals related to the less mundane church calendar, celebrating saints' days and major Christian events like Christmas, which was often the only holiday of the year for early Victorian villagers throughout the land. Christmas had become a typical season of compromise: the Christian rituals of churchgoing counterbalanced the

OPPOSITE **Strolling along the village street kept everyone in touch: Sandford, Yorkshire, in 1875.**

A Victorian Christmas tree in a Somerset school. In working agricultural villages, Christmas was also the start of the 12 days that led to the first bite of the plough into last year's stubble. In some places, local rites were carried out to bring luck to the new crop.

more ancient carnival of feasting, drinking and general rowdiness, tempered in due course by Victorian sentimentality and the introduction of Christmas cards and trees. We can all visualize a Victorian family Christmas, with plum puddings and pumpkin pie, mince tarts and frumenty, spiced ale and home-made wines, robins, carols, holly and snow, carefully masking the pagan midwinter fertility rites of old.

Writing in 1898, a year before his death at the age of 31, Arthur Gibbs claimed that Christmas in his Cotswold hamlet was very similar then to that of a hundred years earlier and that 'Christmas is Christmas still in the heart of old England'. His village's 'humble rejoicings' included 'a grand smoking concert at the club, during which mummers gave an admirable performance of their old play; then a big feed for every man, woman and child of the hamlet (about a hundred souls) was held in the manor house.' Gibbs, it should be noted, lived in the manor house and had been educated at Eton. The family 'received visits from carol singers and musicians of all kinds to the number of seventy-two, reckoning up the total aggregate of the different bands. From villages three and four miles away came bands of children to sing the old, old songs. The brass band, including old grey-haired men who fifty years ago with strings and woodwind led the psalmody at Chedworth Church, come too, and play inside the hall.'

Gibbs was careful to order in four or five 18-gallon casks of beer to keep the atmosphere cheerful, though 'we never saw any man the worse for drink ... but then, we have a butler of the old school.' The whole hamlet ('farmers as well as labourers honoured us') was made welcome at the manor and Gibbs decided to amuse his visitors with his bigotphones – 'delightfully simple contrivances fitted with reed mouthpieces – exact representations in mockery of the various instruments that make up a brass band – but composed of strong cardboard, and dependent solely on the judicious application of the human lips and the skilful modulation of the human voice for their effect.'

His idea was a great success. Young Peregrine, the gamekeeper, chose the bassoon, the carter took the clarionet, the shepherd the French horn, the cowman the trombone, while Gibbs sat at the piano and conducted his orchestra. The players happily improvised *The British Grenadiers*, *A Fine Hunting Day*, *Two Lovely Black Eyes* and even *The Eton Boating Song*. And then they supplied the music for dancing, with 'Miss Peregrine doing the light fantastic round the stone floor of the hall to the tune of *See Me Dance the Polka*; then, too, the stately Mrs Peregrine insisted on our playing *Sir Roger de Coverley* and it was danced with that pomp and ceremony which such occasions alone are wont to show. None of your "kitchen lancers" for us hamlet folk; we leave that kind of thing to the swells and nobs. Tom Peregrine alone was baffled. Whilst his family in general were bowing there, curtseying here, clapping hands and "passing under to the right" in the usual Sir Roger style, he stood in grey homespun of the best material (I never yet saw a Cotswold man in a vulgar chessboard suit), and as he stood he marvelled greatly exclaiming now and then, "Well, I never; this is something new, to be sure!"'

The tradition of country fairs is a long one. Before the 19th century they had ranged from major trade events in market towns to small pedlary fairs held in larger villages, where cottagers would buy household hardware and knick-knacks.

In 1850 almost every village was within ten miles of a market town and villagers thought little of a day-trip walk to the fairs as social outings. There they could watch itinerant tumblers, trick riders, gypsy gymnasts, Punch and Judy shows, dancing bears and monkeys, menageries with lions and tigers; they could sample gingerbread and ale, meet people from a wide area, listen to excitable preachers, clap along with the morris dancers, jig to fiddle music, place bets on the cockfights, dare to have a go with the wrestlers, have their pockets picked, indulge in a good scrap with a neighbouring village and even, occasionally, sell their wives for a shilling or two.

Some fairs also accommodated casual job markets where rural domestic servants and annually employed farmworkers found new posts. The hiring year and the farm year ended at Michaelmas and those who decided to seek new posts would dress in clean clothes and identify their trade by wearing a suitable symbol – perhaps a tuft of wool for a shepherd, a twist of straw for a thatcher, some hair from a cow's tail for a dairy-worker. They would all gather in one place to be eyed by prospective employers before the bargaining began. Agreements were reached verbally, with a handshake and a shilling or so of hiring money or 'fasting' to seal the deal. That done, everybody could go off and enjoy the fair – eat a lot, drink a lot, buy fripperies, brawl, dust up a cheating cheapjack, shy at coconuts, ring the bell on the 'try your strength' machine, listen to the band, court their sweethearts, meet old friends and catch up on all the farm gossip from miles around.

There was still some hiring done at Bicester Fair in the 1870s, though the great days of the fairs were already passing. In 1873 George Dew noticed that 'there was a goodly number of servant girls who were walking about to be hired, but they really of late years have so altered in their style of dress that it is in some cases most difficult to judge as to which is the mistress and which is the servant.'

A dancing bear with its gypsy handlers, c. 1900.

it was the artisans in particular who kept cottage flower-growing alive for future generations, partly for the women's pleasure and partly for the men's urge to compete at the village show. In the heyday of the village, the flower show was often part of a much larger event which included music from the local band, competitive games, a good spread of refreshments and all the little sideshows and stalls of a typical village fête.

The village show was often organized by the parish institute committee of villagers of all classes and occupations, from farmer to farmworker and from blacksmith to schoolmaster. The institute often used its own special meeting-place, typically two rooms well warmed and lighted, provided with newspapers, games and a bagatelle board, and would arrange village hops and concerts to raise funds for good causes. It initiated penny readings, glee clubs, village plays and pageants; it encouraged sewing bees where people gathered together once a week to make items for their bazaars, which also sold home-made preserves and bakes.

The parish institute often ran local cricket and football clubs, too. Many traditional village sports and games had long since been suppressed by the Puritans and the Victorians took the tattered remnants to fashion most of them into genteel games which would have been quite unrecognizable to their earlier players. The landscape gardener Gertrude Jekyll (1843–1932) described at the turn of the century some of the old Whitsun sports, including the traditional fights between rival villages on Whit Monday. For example, the 'Kaffirs' (Cavaliers) of Coneyhurst Hill at Ewhurst in Surrey had a good brawl with the Diamond-topped Roundheads of the Sussex village of Rudgwick on neutral ground at the Donkey Inn in Cranleigh. Miss Jekyll suggested that such rivalry found a safer outlet in cricket, the archetypal village game,

He greatly enjoyed the fair's waxworks show, the performing birds, the sight of a dwarf and, in particular, 'the horses (wooden) and carriages which were driven round by a Steam Engine, while another small engine which worked without cessation drove an organ'. The following year, he noted 'a number of bicycles moving in a circular groove driven by a Steam Engine' and, the weather being poor, 'most of the servant girls were well dabbled in mud, it being so very sloppy'.

Ploughing matches remained a rural attraction well into the 20th century, but the soil can produce more than agricultural crops, and if you think of villages you probably think of cottage gardens bursting with flowers. We owe quite a debt to Victorian cottagers in this respect:

which was already at least 300 years old in Victorian times but was changed out of all recognition when 'official' rules were introduced by a travelling All-England XI who toured by train and spread the gospel according to the MCC.

Arthur Gibbs claimed that cricket in agricultural districts was neglected. 'Men who work day after day in the open air, and to whom a half-holiday is a very rare experience, naturally seek their recreations in less energetic fashion than the noble game of cricket demands of its votaries.' But farmers liked to keep up with county cricket scores, either through newspapers or by attending big matches in the towns, and 80-year-old yeoman farmer Peregrine would go 'mad with excitement' if he was watching his own sons playing village cricket. 'If you take them off the bowling, however much the batsmen appear to relish their attack, he won't forgive you for the rest of the day.' His gamekeeper son usually acted as umpire, wearing a white coat down to his knees and an enormous wide-awake hat and smoking a bad cigar. The village's team included the miller, two of the carpenter's sons, a couple of farmers, a footman, a 'somewhat fat and apoplectic butler' and, as captain, the village curate who stood 6 ft 5 in. tall. The most famous occasion was a visit to play at Edgeworth against the Winson Cricket XI (motto: 'Tired, though United'). The first task was to find the pitch. 'It was known to be in the field in which we stood, because a large red flag floated at one end and proclaimed that somewhere hereabouts was the scene of combat. It was the fat butler, I think, who, after sailing about in a sea of waving butter-cups like a veritable Christopher Columbus, first discovered the stumps among the mowing grass.' Their opponents, farmers and labourers, had hastily chain-harrowed and rib-rolled a small area.

The old game of stoolball is related to cricket and is

possibly the latter's ancestor. In some parts of the country the word 'cricket' describes a low stool, and some claim that stoolball was originally played by milkmaids wielding their three-legged milking stools – a leg for the round bat, and the stool itself as the object of the bowler's aim. Or perhaps not. Joseph Strutt, writing in 1801, described it thus: 'I have been informed that a pastime called stoolball is practised to this day in the northern parts of England, which consists simply in setting a stool upon the ground, and one of the players takes his place before it, while his antagonist, standing at a distance, tosses a ball with the intention of striking the stool, and this it is the business of the former to prevent by beating it away with the hand, reckoning one to the game for every stroke of the ball; if, on

A flower show marquee in Sussex in the 1920s. The village flower show began as an informal competition between gardeners employed on the big estates.

A wrestling picnic in 1897. Wrestling used to be a sport with distinctive local styles: for example, in Cornwall and Devon, there was no ground-wrestling and the participants wore loose linen jackets – Devonians also wore heavy shoes to kick each other's shins.

the contrary, it should be missed by the hand and touch the stool, the players change places; the conqueror at this game is he who strikes the ball most times before it touches the stool.'

Inflated balls or bladders have doubtless been kicked about on village greens for centuries, especially on Shrove Tuesday – a day for all manner of sport but particularly for football, cockthrowing and tugs of war. At Shrovetide in the 1850s in the village streets of Ashbourne, Derbyshire,

they played 'Uppards and Downards'. A white leather ball was booted about for several hours between the Uppards (native villagers born up above the river) and the Downards (those born down of the river). Other natives could play but the only goals which counted were those scored by Uppards or Downards.

Other games were less physically demanding and some villages specialized in tiddlywinks, or marbles (at Tinsley Green for the last three centuries), or conkers, the latter

A village band for all occasions.

more recently at the model village of Ashton, Northamptonshire, which was built in 1900 as a wedding present to his bride by Charles de Rothschild, whose main aim in doing so was to protect the local habitat of a rare species of butterfly. Pigeon-racing was the favourite hobby for cottage metal-workers and Black Country miners, but cockfighting and dogfighting were frowned upon by the large, patriarchal mining companies who instead encouraged less violent entertainments like playing in brass bands.

Music played an important part in village life at all levels and was often self-made. In many parts of England, village bands were commonplace and their music was essential at church services as well as festivals, dances and weddings. The villagers, self-taught musicians who played by ear, collected players' subscriptions to buy instruments which were then loaned to members of the band. The quality of the instruments and their playing was variable, as can be imagined, but did that really matter? The band belonged to the village and was an important part of the social life of the community. Its role was perhaps not so much to please the ear with its harmonies but more to set feet tapping, to enliven an event and to draw attention to it, encouraging the widest possible participation by advertising that it was taking place.

Such bands used a wide range of instruments, though the agricultural villages were usually too poor to forsake their old reeds and winds. With the arrival of portable accordians, however, the 'squeezebox' became an essential accompaniment to rural dancing. Old Isaac Sly, a 'half-witted labouring fellow with a squint in one eye and blind of the other, who at first sight might appear a bad man to meet on a dark night, but is harmless enough when you know him', was a wandering concertina-player who performed inharmoniously at manor houses at Christmas. He would advertise his performances by haunting the lanes carrying an enormous flag.

Isaac also occasionally played at village dances. George Dew greatly resented the 'dancing booths' set up in the village square near the Bell Inn, complaining that he was kept awake by the music, the dancing, the singing, the feasting and the drunkenness of 'young and old, married and single, male and female, of the lower classes' who 'earn their money like horses and spend it like asses.' But it was only once a year, for the Lower Heyford Feast in September. Dew much preferred the band music and flag-waving procession of the Benefit Clubs' annual festivities.

Pianos gradually found their way into middle-class Victorian parlours, but in most villages the favourite instrument cost nothing: it was the human voice, singing local folksongs or contemporary popular songs from penny sheet-music at vicarage concert parties, or rude songs at the inn and the clubhouse, or carols all over the parish, and of course hymns in church and chapel.

A travelling ballad seller, *c.* 1890.

Chapelgoers combined their band music with their thirst for temperance and temperance bands thrived while the movement grew. By 1855 the Band of Hope Union was enrolling children, drumming into them the principles of sobriety and temperance, and the Band of Hope festival became a great social occasion in the village, for adults as well as children and for church as well as chapel. People from other villages joined in the processions down the main street, carrying their banners, singing rousing hymns to the music of the village band, and feasting on tea and buns. Many villages established tea-rooms and coffee-houses as 'dry' alternatives to the inn as social meeting-places.

The umbrella of teetotalism embraced the mid-19th century evolution of working men's clubs in a spirit of self-culture and public good. Villagers had long had their own clubs, particularly those which encouraged thrift – savings clubs, insurance clubs, pig clubs and clothing clubs, for example. The early 19th century was a flourishing time for setting up friendly societies and 'orders', initially as benevolent institutions, and these gradually developed their own insurance schemes and their own rituals, passwords, lodges and other trappings. They ensured that their members could receive cash payments in times of illness or disability in the days of 'no work, no pay'; and gradually there developed special societies for, say, miners, clerks, railway workers and agricultural workers.

The Victorians were deeply concerned with self-improvement. Before the mid 19th century the village's communal meeting-places had been the village green, the church vestry and the inn. The two indoor venues had certain limitations and, apart from the temperance coffee-houses, the Victorians created independent reading rooms as places where 'the artisan, labouring and other poorer classes' could attend lectures and classes to further their education. The reading rooms, often funded by a local benefactor or the squire, were also used for various entertainments but, in the spirit of the times (so to speak), alcohol was strictly forbidden and, as was the Victorian wont, many other restrictions on how the premises could be used were gradually added.

The reading room was the scene for penny readings, usually by the parson (who quite enjoyed the sound of his own mellifluous voice) and it sometimes also housed newspapers and journals for the villagers' browsing. In concept, it was one of the predecessors of the village hall which would eventually offer a much wider scope as the focal meeting-place for the community. Arthur Gibbs described an old ivy-clad building, in the grounds of an old manor house and only a few paces from it, which was used as the village club where 'squire, farmer and labourer are accustomed to meet on equal terms'. He was surprised to find copies of *The Times* and the *Pall Mall Gazette* on the club table in 1898: 'These wonderful specimens of nineteenth-century literature contrast strangely with a place that in many respects has remained unchanged for centuries. There are few labourers in England, even in these days, who have the opportunity – if they will take it – of reading *The Times*' report of every speech made in Parliament.' But they preferred bagatelle and gossip!

Gossip – oh, the joys and skills of village gossip! In 1850 many villages were still inward-looking and more or less cut off from the rest of the world, partly from habit and suspicion but largely because of lack of literacy, lack of communications and inadequate transport. The naturalist W. H. Hudson (1841–1922) was bicycling along a remote Wiltshire lane in the Chalke valley when he noticed a boy

RIGHT **Splashing through puddles at Bratton, Wiltshire. Many country lanes remained as dust or mud even between the wars.**

in a distant field carrying out bird-scaring duties. The boy caught sight of the cyclist and ran at least a quarter of a mile to meet him in the road. Hudson dismounted, and waited, but the boy said nothing. 'Well,' demanded Hudson, 'what do you want?' 'I didn't want anything,' the lad replied. 'Well, what was your object in running?' 'Just to see you pass ....' Such was the isolation that a passing stranger was as worthy of attention to that Wiltshire lad as a white-faced explorer to a jungle tribe.

Hudson was fortunate to have been born late enough for bicycles. In the days of horses and Shanks's pony, country roads were either billowing dust in summer or foot-dragging mud in winter and travel was limited by the state of the roads as much as by the lack of time or incentive to go anywhere. The majority of early Victorian villagers travelled by foot. To understand more about the real psychology and social history of the villager, go nowhere unless you walk there. You will quickly appreciate why villages were self-sufficient and isolated.

Even a hundred years ago most of the inhabitants in more remote villages had been born in the village or one nearby and hardly ever travelled more than ten miles from it. Yet in other areas, especially where industry and mining offered alternative means of employment, there was continual migration throughout the Victorian period. In the Shropshire parish of Highley, for example, some of the workers came from as far away as Northumberland and Newcastle-upon-Tyne, and the great majority of children left the village by the time they were adolescents, usually with their parents who were following new work opportunities. The 1861 census showed that the new railways were having a considerable influence on Highley's population, a quarter of whom were railway navvies and their families staying in the parish temporarily, including navvies born in 23 different counties. George Walter, for example, was

born in Buckinghamshire and had worked in Doncaster, Caerphilly and Worcestershire before coming to Highley at the age of 33. Several navvies' children had been born in France while their fathers helped to build the Paris-to-Rouen and other northern French railways.

Villages which happened to lie on major routes in

LEFT **Tramps brewing up at the roadside.**

of home, leading to the creation and upkeep of a network of local footpaths which were trod with purpose, not for leisure. Every track led to where people had to go in the course of their daily business. Sometimes that 'business' was not to the farmer's liking. Thomas Garne (1784–1851), a yeoman farmer in the Cotswolds, so resented the crowds using paths across his cornfields to the local Bibury racecourse that he sprinkled red sheep-raddle powder on the crop to deter at least the crinolined ladies. His resentment was understandable: the races attracted considerable crowds and their unthinking damage to his crops and livestock was no doubt substantial. The races were at their heyday at the beginning of the 19th century and an old yeoman farmer remembered that Bibury village shopkeepers in the 1830s would let their own bedrooms to racegoers and sleep on the shop counter, with their families under it.

Throughout the century, country lanes were well used by the countrywide network of carriers, wagoners and packhorse stringers or jaggers. Generally rutted cart-tracks – with *three* ruts (the middle one trodden by the horse, and no doubt well dunged) – they echoed peacefully to the deliberate clopping of cart-horses, the wheels creaking and the harness bells jingling cheerily so that you could hear them coming and make for a convenient passing place. The lanes were lazily busy with cows mooching their way to be milked, plough teams returning home, wayward pigs being driven to market, sheep being brought down from the hills, and sometimes more exotic creatures. The *Salisbury and Winchester Journal* recorded an exciting report about the lead horse of the London-to-Exeter mail coach being attacked by a lioness. She had escaped from a travelling menagerie camping nearby and was pulled off the lacerated horse by a large Newfoundland dog.

Itinerants such as one-man bands, wandering fiddlers,

various parts of the country profited from the traffic in long-distance coaches, carriages and carts and kept in touch with the outside world. Byway villages, however, remained isolated; intermarriage was rife and the inbred rustic 'idiot' was a familiar local character. Most people continued to work, visit and court within walking distance

ABOVE **Drovers taking cattle through Modbury in Devon.**

ABOVE RIGHT **A pair of one-man bands in Taplow, Buckinghamshire.**

acrobats, gypsies with dancing bears, organ-grinders, the hurdy-gurdy man and his Punch and Judy show, all wandered the lanes on their way to the fairs and resorts for the summer season. There were all manner of small traders, many of them setting up their portable workshops on the village green or calling at individual dwellings. There were migrant workers on their way to join harvest gangs or pick fruit or dig potatoes; there were numerous tramps and gypsies, but above all there were the villagers – people gathering firewood and blackberries or making verge hay; field labourers walking to work bearing their nuncheon firkins; gleaners coming home with their sacks; people dressed in their best to visit relatives; lovers strolling; children playing – everybody ready to chat at the gates they passed and with those they happened to meet. The lanes belonged to people, not vehicles, and that was still true in the 1920s and beyond. The lanes and the village street were an important part of everyday life, and were full of people willing to pause for a gossip at the slightest excuse.

The old way of life gave plenty of opportunity for gossiping – in the lane, in the street, at the gate, on the green, at the smithy, in the shop, after church or chapel, at socials and games, at the club or in the alehouse, and of course at the parish pump. Gossip coloured and broadened individuals' lives by embracing those of others; gossip was the verbal journalism that knitted the many strands of community life.

The development of what eventually became cheap, rapid public transport changed village life radically and permanently by destroying its introversion. England's first main railway routes had been laid during the 1830s; and a boom in the 1840s led to rapid railway-building all over the country which continued throughout the century. By 1850 the railways were already dominant over canals and roads for freight and long-distance passenger traffic.

It was the railways that first liberated villagers and opened new horizons for them, directly and indirectly. While new lines were being built, agricultural workers found a choice of employment right on their doorsteps: they could, for a while, become navvies; later some joined the permanent railway staff; and, eventually, they could travel by train to places where opportunities and wages were far better than in the village. By the 1870s, cheap fares were available for workers.

Crossing the countryside on the new long-distance lines, many urban travellers noticed the countryside for the first time, while employers realized that there was a large pool of cheap labour out there, waiting to be tapped. Instead of only through trains, there were country trains stopping at frequent intervals at established rural halts. Although many of the rural branch lines were not built until the later decades of the century and some were financed by the local nobility – usually in their own interests – in due course the country train had advantages for the local population as well.

To begin with railways were designed essentially to carry freight in bulk. Country stations handled local produce sent out to new markets and also commodities bought in from the mills, mines and towns for local consumption. Those villages lucky enough to have a station depot of their own (a relatively small number) began to flourish, though often the village's station was a

LEFT **A cycling knife-grinder and his pedlar wife in 1905.**

mile away. New buildings began to drift towards stations, stretching out the village, changing its shape and centre of gravity.

Farmers began to use their local railway station to travel to town on business as well as to transport livestock for the markets and churns of milk for town dairies. Graziers and cattle-dealers, horse-dealers and wagoners travelled with their animals; herdsmen and hedgers and labourers of all kinds gradually began to travel to work by train. Local hunts, too, benefited from a nearby country station or halt: riders, horses and hounds could travel to the meet by train.

As a source of passenger traffic the country stations were always a drain on resources – from the railway companies' point of view, that is. For the villagers, they were the gateway to the rest of the world. Eventually, the majority of villagers found themselves within walking distance of a station and they began to use the train for local trips to the nearest town on market day. Some villagers were more adventurous. In the 1890s, Tom Partridge related the hilarious adventure of Roger Plowman, a Cotswold native who decided to take a trip to 'Lunnon' by train from 'Cizzeter' to see 'Sairy Jane'. All the village knew of his intention, and warned him he was sure to be murdered along the way, or at least taken in. So Roger walked to Cirencester station and saw that people

BELOW RIGHT **Train and staff at Swanage, Dorset, in 1895.**

BELOW **Building the Whitby/Stockton railway line, c. 1875.**

were paying money for bits of pasteboard. He followed their example but was nonplussed when asked, 'Fust, second or thurd?' First, of course, he said – he did not want to keep Sairy Jane waiting. The ticket-seller demanded more than a pound, but Roger had been told the fare would be only eight shillings. Luckily the man then told him that third class would reach London in the same time as first. Roger climbed into a row of carriages waiting for London and 'off we went as fast as a racehoss . . . . Never in aal me life did I go at such a rate under and awver bridges and droo holes in the 'ills. We wur soon at Swindon, wur a lot wur at work as black as tinkers.' At Swindon he had to change trains and looked for a bite to eat, ordering bread and bacon from 'sum nation good-looking gurls a-waitin'.' But all they gave him was sausages with thin bread and butter. Then he ordered a quart of ale but heard a whistle and a grunt from the steamer – out he went 'an', begum! he wur off.' Poor Roger! His fork still in a sausage and his mouth full, he waved at a chap to stop the train but everybody laughed. So he went back to his meal and ordered a bottle of ale, which fizzed all over the place – she had given him 'Moses's shampane, at seven shillin's an' sixpence a bottle.' His final bill of 'thirteen scaramouches' also included the cost of seven sausages and two dozen slices of bread and butter. He would always remember 'Swindle-um stashum'.

Mavis Budd, whose country childhood in the 1920s was very like that of the 1880s, travelled with her family by train once a year, to the market town of Petersfield, Hampshire, nine miles away, for the fun of shopping, mingling with the crowds, listening to the Salvation Army band and, above all, buying fresh cod from the 'Lovely Grub' fishmonger from Portsmouth.

The trip was undertaken with a due sense of great occasion which began long before the three-mile walk across the wild common to the station, with Mother undertaking urgent last-minute chores, Father calming the dog and Mavis fretting that they would miss the train. Her impatience increased during the walk, as her parents sauntered along, deliberately 'pausing to look at the view, a new hayrick, or a gap where a tree had been cut and which they hadn't noticed before. They discussed this and that, stopped to shake sand out of their shoes and to gossip to people we met.' But they always arrived at the station in good time and Mother bought the tickets while Father 'pottered about in the station yard, looking at whatever there was to look at, and probing about among the wagons and farm equipment which lay about. The station was

The country station was used as a major freight centre. Here strawberries are being loaded at Swanwick in Hampshire, c. 1900.

small and really much less like a railway station and much more like a smallholding. There were flourishing vegetables on the banks and wherever there was earth to grow things in. Chickens roamed the line. Goats were tethered in the sidings. Lines of washing hung along the platform at the far end, and the garbled voices of ducks came from the back of the waiting-room. We hadn't been waiting long before a bell clanged. The goats danced in a sudden circle. The hens clucked and fluttered with panic, while the ducks set up a long chorus of disturbance. "That means she's left Midhurst," said Mother. "Now you can begin to watch for her."' On the journey home, laden with their shopping, there was the occasional problem – like the day that the engine went off without its carriages!

As rail travel became faster and cheaper, and as wages increased and working hours decreased, more and more could afford the time and fares for the journey. The real mass appeal of the railway lay in the cheap excursion trains of the second half of the century – travel for leisure rather than work. From the village to the city, from the town to the seaside and countryside, and from town and country to the big sports events and exhibitions, people began to flock in large numbers on the excursion trains.

Temporary escapes from the village for pleasure grew rapidly in Victorian times, though generally the participants took most of the village with them on such outings, initially by horsedrawn wagonette, to sample the magic atmosphere of the seaside. Little seaside bathing villages developed into resorts, served from the early years of the century by coaches, canal boats and estuary and coastal steamships, but it was the railways that brought the workers *en masse* and introduced to the masses the idea of spending holidays away from home.

Excursions helped to alter the focus of the village, turning it outwards, away from the green and the parish

OPPOSITE **A full Lincolnshire wagon ready for a village outing from Bassingham.**

LEFT
Freddy Edmonds, a successful wagonette proprietor in 1912.

pump. Villagers took trains to watch prize fights, horse-racing and public executions. In 1848 more than 100,000 spectators turned up to watch the public hanging of a multiple murderer in Liverpool; in 1851 the Great Exhibition attracted six million visitors to its celebration of the nation's industrial and commercial success, many of them agricultural workers travelling to London by excursion trains from all over the country; and during the hard winter of 1878–9 large numbers of skaters took the train to go skating on frozen flooded valleys at Somerton in Oxfordshire.

The Victorian country station grew busy and its station-master, who worked a 13-hour day, soon became an honorary member of the local community and often a well-respected one. His experience tended to be broader than that of those born and raised in the village. He was often active in village affairs, perhaps as churchwarden, or as a member of the parish institute and, in due course, the parish council. He was an outsider who brought new ideas into the village.

Many a villager enjoyed the simple pleasure of watching the evening train come in, and the station bridge became another focal point where people could meet casually and chat. The station also became a centre for means of communication other than trains. The electric telegraph system, by which messages concerning railway matters were passed down the line to other stations, was soon used to pass messages on behalf of the post office with the station-master acting as agent for postal telegrams. In the 1870s the writer Richard Jefferies described a very modern young 'bicycle farmer' who thought it such a waste of valuable time riding round his large farms that he toyed with the idea of installing an adapted military field telegraph system, using a pony to unroll the reel of wire so that the busy farmer could sit in his office all day, issuing instructions to his workforce by telegraph.

The combination of telegraph and railway became a means of spreading information about job opportunities elsewhere, tempting workers away from the villages. The railways also introduced a new concept of time. Before, everything had happened slowly and time was relative: people kept local time, regardless of what time it was thought to be elsewhere. There had been no need to conform to other people's schedules until the railway network demanded standardization for its timetables. Gradually villagers came to accept 'railway time' (Greenwich time) throughout the country and everyone who had a clock could set it to coincide with everyone else's.

The rapid trend towards uniformity accelerated with the distribution, by rail, of newspapers – the natural extension of village gossip and compulsive spurs to learning to read. The availability of local papers from nearby towns to an increasing number of literate villagers helped reduce the village's sense of isolation, linking it to the outside world – a trend which increased with the distribution of national newspapers and weekly journals into the villages. Rural people began to read of national events and to absorb national attitudes. Advertisements in the national press encouraged them to share urban fashions, tastes and opinions. By the end of the Victorian era the village's protective shell of isolation and introversion was cracking and the day of the 'global village' loomed.

CHAPTER 3

The Changing Village

The ability to escape from the village was one of the most striking reasons for the transformation of English village life after 1850. The improvements in communications opened a two-way gate which allowed villagers greater physical and intellectual freedom and also enabled many more outsiders from the towns to move into villages.

Several other factors played their part in changing village life. The increase in population forced many off the land to seek higher wages elsewhere, while technological improvements reduced the actual number of men needed to work the land. Compulsory education led many to be dissatisfied with the limitations of village life, while war offered new horizons to some and unsettled many.

But perhaps the most important agent of change (and an effect as well as a cause) was the rapid urbanization of England, which filtered into every village in the land, significantly altering people's attitudes and sending the village careering towards the anonymity and uniformity of standardization.

Urbanization went hand in hand with a rapid rise in population. In 1801, the year of the first regular ten-year census, the population of Britain was about 11 million.

Only one in five people lived in towns. In 1851, for the first time in Britain's history, more than half the country's population lived in towns rather than villages. The 1850s formed a pivotal decade in which the balance between town and country was irredeemably tilted townwards. In the 1860s the rural population was plummeting as workers fled from the land, villages and poverty, and thereafter the ratio of townsfolk over countryfolk accelerated rapidly.

When Queen Victoria died in 1901, the population had doubled during her reign to 37 million. By 1947, 85 per cent of the population was urban in situation and an even larger proportion was urban in outlook, but there were still about a million farmworkers. Today, the total population of the UK is nearly 57 million and less than 300,000 people are directly employed in farming, forestry and fishing.

An 1850s villager would, of course, be amazed at the startling changes that have occurred over the past century – especially the depopulation of the land. Fields are no longer full of horses and hand-labourers, many villages are ghostly quiet and empty during the day, motor vehicles rather than people fill the lanes, and most of those who now live in rural villages are from urban backgrounds. It is the urban influence that is shaping the modern countryside

and the modern village. The land is no longer the home of the countryman and in large parts of the country it is rare to find traditional families who are village-born.

The imbalance between town and country became more marked during the later 19th century as dissatisfied field-labourers and their families drifted into the towns in growing numbers, or the rural young took the bolder step of emigrating to a brave new world in the Americas and Australasia. As communications with the world beyond the village improved, urban goods and ideas were brought into its heart and hastened the demise of local craft-workers and traders. People began to buy goods mass-produced in the towns or imported from overseas, rather than handmade individual items produced by the village shoemaker or joiner, while the traditional cottage industries by which villagers supplemented low incomes were being swallowed up by the industrial giants of town factories and mills, making the villagers' output obsolete. The village was being economically absorbed by the town, becoming but a glint in the town merchant's eye, losing its independence and losing its work.

As its horizons broadened, the 19th-century village became more cosmopolitan in its outlook and demands, at the expense of its working heart and sense of identity. The change from self-sufficiency and productive independence to the anonymity of mass-market consumerism took place largely in Victoria's reign, and by its close the towns had won. Most people were by then finally divorced from the land, divorced from the realities of nature, divorced from the traditions of village life and frequently hostile to those who worked on the land.

In the 1880s and 1890s, with a growing amount of leisure time, town-dwellers were already becoming tourists in the countryside. Day-trippers, delighting in their visits, were glad to scurry back to the reassuring familiarity of the

town for their 'real' life. Later, in search of a 'lost heritage' and with an unrealistic dream of country living, some would come back to live in the village, but the thread had been broken and townspeople unwittingly came back as invaders rather than as lost sheep. In doing so, they were in danger of ruining the very thing they sought, if they even knew what that was.

ABOVE **Gleaning was an economic necessity: a diligent family could gather enough grain to keep them in bread for several months.**

The little Wylye Valley village of Stockton, in Wiltshire, illustrates several facets of the changing village. Between the first national census in 1801 and the 1930s its

OPPOSITE **Taking a break after stooking the sheaves.**

population was always within two dozen either side of 200, and by 1937 there were 186 people, living in 56 houses. The most notable change during this period was in occupations. In 1847, the parson noted that there were 46 cottagers, three carpenters, three shoemakers, two grocers, two blacksmiths, a pig-dealer, a wheelwright, a butcher, a maltster, a curate and a parson, a beershop keeper, and the tailor John Dyer who sat crosslegged in his window at number 22 and who also played the cello in church.

In 1930 the picture was very different and many people seemed to have become servants: there were three man-servants, five maids, seven gardeners and a chauffeur at Stockton House; five maids, three gardeners and a groom at Long Hall; five or six other houses employing a maid and a gardener or groom; and elsewhere another six gardeners, two grooms, a butler, a houseman and a gamekeeper. There were also six farmers (one of whom was also the coal merchant), a clerk of works, a rector, an innkeeper, a motorbus driver, and three railwaymen.

Tom Farley, who died in World War I, was the last of a family who had lived in the village for five centuries. The Fleming family, who had been carpenters there since the 17th century, had also disappeared, and the Giles family, blacksmiths since 1809, had ceased that trade entirely. Yet old Mrs Giles, looking back 60 years to the village she remembered in the 1870s, said that it had changed little. She remembered her fellow villagers then as 'genuine Wiltshire people, friendly, contented, and happy, always ready to lend a helping hand. Everyone joined in dancing, sliding, skating in the meadows, or picnics on the downs.' No occasion was complete without dancing to an accordion, concertina, fiddle, whistle pipe or mouth organ or, failing all, the dancers' own singing and whistling. Music, she stressed, had been part of everyday life in the village. In winter, they turned the smithy into a hall for singing (and

boxing) and 'made music' with the sledge and anvil. Most of the village came to watch it by the light of a stable lantern, perching themselves on planks set across barrels. In July, there was an annual village feast signalling a whole week of 'jollity' – several villagers would obtain temporary licences to sell beer from their own homes ('tea was too expensive'), stalls were set up all along the village street selling sweets, cakes and ginger ale, while Charlie Topp from Codford sold cockles and winkles, and the first new potatoes were dug from every garden and allotment for the feast itself. On Shrove Tuesday singing children paraded around the village, and again on May Day carrying their garlands. On Whit Monday the village club and its band marched up to the big house and spent the evening dancing on its lawns. At Christmas there were carol singers and mummers and at Harvest Home the farmers in the 1870s were still laying on the traditional harvest feasts. There would be village fêtes at the slightest excuse, whether for local events like the return of a general from the Sudan or national ones like coronations or royal weddings.

But in truth, the 1930s village in which old Mrs Giles lived with her good memories was very different from that of the 1870s. The agricultural base had dwindled drastically and the bond between villagers and the land had been broken. And it was this – the loss of touch with the all-powerful reality of nature – that was the fundamental change in village life, and what is today's villager cannot hope to recapture.

⁓

In the generation or two since 1850, then, village life had been changed largely by outside influences, rather than by evolution from within. Yet the same queen remained on the throne during the dying century and many of the familiar activities and attitudes persisted, albeit diluted.

In theory, democracy came to the villagers during the last two decades of the century – long after it had reached the towns – inevitably hastening changes in attitude as well as practical matters. In 1884, some two million agricultural workers at last became enfranchized, five decades later than town labourers. Many promptly voted Liberal in defiance of the Tory squires and farmers. Four years later, county councils were created, followed in 1894 by rural district and parish councils. Between them these two bodies would take over many of the functions of the squire, the open vestry meetings and the various offices which villagers had performed in the past.

The working life of the village was changing, too. Many cottage industries had collapsed, many crafts were dying out and many agricultural jobs had vanished. There were still a few hiring fairs in the 1890s for those on annual contracts, but the most obvious changes in the fields were the increasing use of machinery and the disappearance of agricultural gangs. Women and children were no longer a common sight in the fields after the 1870s and even the familiar itinerant gangs of seasonal casual and skilled labourers had dwindled. The continual drift of people from rural areas, which had been the almost unremarked trend for some three generations, became a noted problem for farmers in the 1890s. The agricultural dominance of village work had waned and farming itself was in the depths of a major, long-lasting depression.

No wonder the villager got on his bike, literally. The humble bicycle was a symbol of the villager's new personal freedom to leave the village physically as well as emotionally, and to pedal wherever and whenever the urge arose, without having to rely on the timetables of trains and carriers. The safety bicycle, with wheels of equal size,

Mechanization was displacing the field crowds: inventions reduced the needs for village labour. This is a steam-thresher in Rutland in the 1920s.

arrived in the 1880s and a bicycle boom began: cycle touring started to become popular in the 1880s and was all the rage in the 1890s as the machines developed rapidly to please the public and entice the tourer. The middle classes took to bicycles with gusto and the pages of *The Field*, the 'gentleman's paper', were full of suggestions for long-distance journeys and ideas about fashionable wear.

47

Arthur Gibbs prophesied that the bicycle would probably 'cause a larger demand for country houses' as it 'brings places sixty miles apart within our immediate neighbourhood. Let the south wind blow,' he cried, 'and we can be at quaint old Tewkesbury, thirty miles away, in less than three hours. A northerly gale will land us at the "Blowing-stone" and the old White Horse of Berkshire with less labour than it takes to walk a mile. Yet in the old days these twenty miles were a great gulf fixed between the Gloucestershire natives and the "chawbacons" over the boundary. Their very language is as different as possible.'

Although initially bicycles were confined to middle-class touring, they were so practical that they soon became an essential part of country life. George Dew, who made his rounds on a pony called Tom in the 1870s and later by pony-and-trap, decided in 1881 that he was not getting enough exercise and bought himself an 18-guinea tricycle, selling Tom to a roadside gypsy for £4. Dew, who first learned to ride a bicycle, with difficulty, in 1871, remarked: 'I never saw one till about 12 or 18 months ago, and now there are several in Heyford.' He was so thrilled with the experience of mastering the art that he was soon travelling more than 25 miles a day for work purposes, and then riding it again for the pleasure of social visits in the evening, despite the roads being 'abominably muddy and bad'.

Bicycles took you anywhere your legs could pedal but twice as fast as walking there, and they were cheap to run if you could afford the initial outlay. In Edwardian times, for those who could not, the old 'ride-and-tie' system of sharing ponies was transferred to the bicycle: you rode your shared bike for a certain distance and left it in the hedge for your mate while you continued on foot. The new rider overtook you in due course and, in turn, left the bike in another hedge further on – more like leapfrog than a bicycle made for two. Nobody stole it and there was hardly any traffic to knock you into the ditch.

Bicycles became the workers' 'ponies', helping them to travel that much further and faster, thus widening the choice of employment. Villagers also discovered that bicycles opened up new social possibilities – they could look further afield for marriage partners and general entertainment.

Although the ability to travel and the spread of literacy had widened villagers' horizons, entertainments were still relatively simple. The village band remained popular and there was a golden age for bands from the 1880s until the 1920s. In 1899 there were about 40,000 amateur bands in Britain.

My own north Sussex village, a small, scattered parish of a few hundred people, had its own one-tune brass band in late Victorian times. It also had its own black-and-white minstrels, whose concert sheet for 1896 names relatives of the bandsmen and other names locally familiar today. The programme records that the proceeds from the concert were to be devoted to 'the completion of the Purchase of the American Organ'. The troupe became quite famous in Sussex, entertaining seaside crowds at distant Bognor Regis as well as those at local villages' festivals and carnivals, and raising money for charity wherever they went. Les Vale's father was one of them, his face blacked with burnt cork and playing 'a big instrument, a horn five feet high – big brass thing like a cow horn'. At a carnival one year he was cut over the eye by pennies thrown by some lads outside an inn and bore this noble scar for the rest of his life.

The problem with village society was that everybody already knew everybody else and, for the young in particular, social events palled when they simply met the same people at each one. It is little wonder that, as

OPPOSITE **Tourists at the crossroads at Bucklebury, Berkshire, in 1900, with the Blade Bone Inn in the distance. Bicycles brought tourists to the countryside but then took villagers away from the village.**

transport gradually became more widely available in rural areas, the young and not-so-young headed to the towns for their entertainment – to town dances rather than village hops and, later, to the alluring flicker of the cinema screen.

Yet there was still plenty of life in the village, and Queen Victoria's Diamond Jubilee (1897) was a good excuse for building new venues. Arthur Gibbs remarked acidly that the parish council of his Gloucestershire hamlet 'seriously proposed to erect a "Jubilee Hall" of *red* brick in the village. Anything for a change, you see; these people would not be mortals if they did not love a change.' His horror was not with the idea of a hall but with the neglect of the local building material, grey limestone from the Cotswold hills.

In Surrey, the village worthies of Chobham decided to build a hall in honour of the Queen's Golden Jubilee in 1887. This was one of the earliest purpose-built community halls in the country and its charitable trustees included the vicar, a couple of yeoman farmers and a provisions merchant. The hall was built on a field donated by a local landowner and was an immediate success, its facilities, soon extended by the addition of a two-roomed parish institute which was used as a library and for the educational, recreative and other benefits of the villagers. The institute, open to any local man aged over 15, became a popular men's club where they played 'interesting games and competitions', had access to 'disused magazines, periodicals and pictorials', and were provided with billiards, bagatelle, draughts, dominoes and card-games in comfortable surroundings – for only a shilling a month.

The hall was also the venue for dramatic entertainments, concerts, temperance lectures, choral recitals, recitations, glees, band music, shadow-picture shows, public lectures, regular mothers' meetings, technical education classes, and the annual parochial tea with songs, banjo music and children's choruses. At Christmas there was the Sunday school treat with a decorated tree, a conjurer and presents for each child. The parochial Slate Club had celebratory share-outs in the hall after a supper ('the Phonograph proved a great attraction and was evidently a novelty to most of those present . . .') and there were gatherings for the choir, the bell-ringers, the Temperance Society and the annual old people's dinner.

Public 'penny readings' in the hall were always crowded. By 1913 villagers were paying a penny for admission but threepence to reserve a seat and it seems that 'an overwhelming majority of our young bloods were exemplary in their conduct, in spite of the fact that they were asked, and readily responded, to give up their seats to older people' – but some of the young 'whose spirits are irrepressible' were courteously banned.

In 1916 a baby welfare centre was opened in the hall, offering 'such strengthening foods as Virol, Glaxo, Malt and Cod Liver Oil' at cost price for mothers of infants under school age, and there were wartime concerts to raise funds for Christmas presents for soldiers serving overseas. But World War I was to bring more changes to the English village and, indeed, some would say that it finally closed the chapter on the traditional community of villagers working for and within their village.

OPPOSITE **Roasting an ox in Dorset to celebrate the coronation of King Edward VII in 1902. Royal jubilees and coronations were typical excuses for entertainments to add to annual village events.**

War

The two World Wars proved to be watersheds for village life. Although their horizons had broadened, villages before 1914 were still contained communities and in some areas the squire, in one guise or another, enjoyed considerable influence right up to World War II. But the wars precipitated change. The village might lose many of its sons, either temporarily during their time of service, or permanently as war casualties or because the village boy's taste of life beyond the parish had whetted his appetite and encouraged him to seek a new life elsewhere. Men who went abroad to fight for their homeland came back changed and dissatisfied with the old way of life.

World War I burst suddenly and dramatically right into the heart of village life. Relating the story of Lord Iveagh's estate village of Elveden in Suffolk, George Martelli described a scene common to many wartime village schools and halls. The squire, rector and perhaps a retired local general together with the local MP as a guest speaker would sit on the flag-draped platform. The seats in the front rows would be empty – as for so many village gatherings – while the old folks and women sat in the middle rows and the men of military age at the very back.

The squire would invite volunteers to step forward and, after an awkward silence, the first farmboy would stand up, to ribald comments from his mates, and make his way to the platform. Others would gradually follow and the session usually closed to the strains of 'We don't want to lose you, but we think you ought to go . . . .'

The billeting of troops in villages had a major impact in some regions. In Wiltshire, vast tracks of land were taken over by the military for the establishment of camps – tents at first and then huts – creating small towns on what hitherto had been farmland. Local villages now resounded to the echo of marching boots and the camps were filled with soldiers flocking to the temporary shops, cafés and barbers set up specially to serve their needs. For many villagers, the influx of so many strangers in their midst was both disrupting and unwelcome.

In the fields, village women and older children worked beside members of the Women's Land Army – formed in 1917 to make up the depleted number of agricultural workers who had joined the services. The need for extra hands on the land also resulted in urban women and public schoolboys being encouraged to take working holidays on farms – picking hops or gathering the flax

OPPOSITE **A wartime group of temporary landworkers.**

which now blanketed many fields with its morning haze of blue flowers.

World War I also had the effect of revitalizing (if only temporarily) many rural crafts and old farming practices. The arts of herbalism and hedgerow cookery were rediscovered in order to make up for national shortages of medicine and food. Though medicinal herbs were grown in large quantities, the greatest demand was for food. With the German U-boat blockade limiting the amount of food Britain could import, every inch of ground was forced into cultivation and everyone – from the squire and his wife to the poorest cottager – contributed their labour and forgotten skills to producing more food. Once again there was a huge, busy army of people at work in the countryside.

The changing village street: electricity poles, cars and advertisements are starting to appear.

The physical faces of many villages were deliberately changed after the war. The government encouraged the building of 'homes for heroes' and the establishment of smallholdings to help rebuild rural life. Old cottages were demolished to make way for new housing and by the 1930s new bungalows were strung along roads leading out of villages. The shape of the traditional village had changed.

The newcomers, more demanding and articulate than the indigenous villagers, helped to encourage the belated provision of services to rural areas, but they were a long time in coming. In my own village there was no electricity or mains water until 1949 or 1950 and this was typical of many villages. It was not until 1953 that electricity came to rural areas on a major scale. Before then, villagers cooked on solid-fuel ranges and for light relied on oil and paraffin lamps. Yet the pattern varied: in Castor, Northamptonshire, the gas street-lamps erected in 1900 were converted to electricity in 1931. By the end of that year, Castor also had an automatic telephone exchange although home telephones in rural areas were limited to the middle classes for a long while, though the familiar red kiosks appeared in the villages between the wars. In the 1930s farmers began to recognize how useful these newfangled instruments could be, but it was not until after World War II that telephones came to the cottagers.

It was after World War I that county councils first began to provide rural library services and books were deposited in accessible buildings such as the reading room, village school, hall, vicarage or even the pub, though often the total stock of books was no greater than the number of people in the village (one each!). The site of a village's 'library' was identified by what became the familiar sign of a flaming torch of knowledge, often seen outside the schools or the many village halls which were built to commemorate the village's war dead. The hall movement really

gathered strength after a National Council, formed in 1919 to bring together a richly varied collection of voluntary groups and clubs operating in the villages, decided that parish councils were not active enough. Slightly to their surprise, villagers suddenly found their social lives being 'improved' by people who talked about generating 'community action' in the villages as if it was a new idea rather than the age-old basis of village life.

Women's Institutes, which had been 'brightening the lives' of women in the villages since 1915, encouraging them to boost home food production by direct action as part of the war effort, set a trend for what would become, in the 1930s, a positive plethora of initialled bodies determined to 'help' the village, whether it liked it or not. There was already a strong tendency for the social life of the village to be run by the more forceful and usually better educated 'settlers', and between the wars the countryside was being visited by evening lecturers from the urban Workers' Educational Association, or by actors and musicians worthily bringing their art into the barns and halls, organizing arts festivals, music societies, choral societies and drama groups. And in their wake there came a veritable rash of 'social services' as motor cars became increasingly available.

The Rural Industries Bureau, for example, aimed to bring new jobs into the villages to counteract the high level of unemployment. 'Rural Community Councils' began to investigate country health services, rural housing, arrangements for refuse disposal, the effects of industrialization, the need for recreational opportunities among the village's young, and so on. Poor villagers! Committees everywhere! All those well-meaning sets of initials, usually springing from urban areas, were usurping what might usefully have been the role of the parish councils (formed in the 1890s) and had once been the role of the parson and the squire.

Culture for the countryside: 'The Actor' and his caravan in a Sussex field in the 1920s.

The post-1918 village became somewhat self-conscious and worthy with its reading rooms, clubs and whist drives and the gradual revival by the newcomers of village cricket and football teams whose pitches had been given over to sheep or ploughed up for wartime food production. Every village lucky enough to have a hall, however humble (like my own village's fondly remembered Chicken Shed, which originally it had been), had its fortnightly dances in spite of the increasing lure of home gramophones and wirelesses or town cinemas. The halls fought back: they had their own village cinemas, hiring a fresh bill of reels every week.

On the whole, village entertainments became more middle class, reflecting the social changes in the village. Writing in the 1920s and 1930s Humphrey Pakington described typical 'scenes and enactments inseparably associated with the English village', including members of the WI taking tea on the rectory lawn, the gentry and farmfolk attending church on Sunday morning, children in crocodile file leaving the school, lovers strolling by the

Findon Fair on the South Downs in Sussex in the 1920s.

stream, lads gathering around the pump, the brogue-shod lady of the manor exercising her small dogs, an old man leaning over the sty-wall to chat to the pigs, handwritten notices advertising village events in the shop window, men in muddy boots quaffing ale by the pub's fireside, their bikes propped up outside, ducks gossiping on the pond and sleeping unmolested by the roadside, a church fête with home-made produce and entertainments.

Here and there a few of the old customs persisted and there were countless photographers who, in the interwar years, had little compunction about deliberately posing 'rustic' characters doing 'rustic' things like dwile-flonking, making hay or wearing their smocks. Many photographs in collections from this period, and many Edwardian ones too, provide false images of rural life, very few having been taken by working villagers.

Yet there were still some genuine rural celebrations, such as the few remaining livestock fairs. The little village of Findon on the South Downs holds its annual sheep fair even now and you can spend the day there breathing in the lanolin smell of sheep, listening to the babble of bleats and watching the haggling. It has changed a lot, though, since Victorian times when the animals poured over the slopes in huge, flowing flocks like cream spilling down the hills.

In the 1830s the whole of Sussex and half of Kent came to this fair on Nepcote Green, where 3000 sheep filled the wattle pens. By the late 19th century it had become the village's great annual holiday: there were other livestock, sideshows, a travellers' pleasure fairground and the annual hiring fair as well as the sheep market. By the 1920s there were 10,000 sheep at Findon and Clem Fowler, an auctioneer who attended his first fair in 1917, remembers the animals 'coming over the hill like small clouds in the dawn mist' from miles around, driven over the day before to spend the night in local fields. After the sale, vast droves of sheep were drifted over the Downs and dropped off in lots at the farms of those who had bought them. Most of the sheep walked both ways – it was not until 1928 that the first lorries came to transport some of them. The auctioneers shepherded many lots to the nearest railway station, however, and in 1925 there were so many that Southern Railways provided a special shunting engine to pull 80 truckloads of sheep for dispersal to buyers too far away for the drovers.

For the first three or four decades of our century, the rural railway station was still an important part of everyday life. Everywhere, the railway brought new people to rural areas, either passing through or doing business or taking day-trips into the countryside. And the trains brought seasonal migrant workers out from the towns to help with the harvest – there were, for example, annual 'Hop-picker Specials' giving city folk a taste of country life on a working holiday, and railway cattle-trucks loaded with Irish harvest gangs from Liverpool were sent out over a wide area.

By 1939, however, the heyday of the rural railway had begun to wane as motorized transport once again brought goods and passengers back to the roads. Between the wars the rural bus firmly put the country train back in its place. Village buses were more convenient than trains and they stopped where people needed them to stop.

In trains, people read, sleep or stare out of the window – not at all the style of village society. Villagers took joyfully to their country bus as a major lifeline and an essentially social service carrying people on very local journeys. On buses they could gossip, stop a while to pick mushrooms and blackberries or pause to let the geese amble across the road. Each bus and bus-stop was a little village in itself and everybody knew the driver as a personal friend. The country bus was the motorized version of the old horse-and-cart village carrier, who simply modernized his existing business and became a busman.

By the 1920s, there were also 'sharrybangs', which feature quite often in old village photographs, either collecting half the village for communal outings or bringing tourists from the cities. Some villagers did well from the charabanc trade. Maud Bridger's grandfather catered for the trippers at Waggoners Wells, a Hampshire beauty spot, and Theresa Grace's mother decided in the 1920s to serve teas in her remote downland village when her husband was made redundant. The family laughed at mother's idea – only the gentry and the local doctor had cars and nobody was likely to pass their way by chance. But mother put a 'TEAS' sign in the front window and a pair of cycling tourists arrived thankfully at the door

A hop-picking scene in Herefordshire in the 1920s. Hop-pickers camped in fields and barns, enjoyed fresh air and good company, and worked hard, being paid by the bushel.

within half an hour. The new teashop appeared in the Cyclists' Touring Club guides and was soon inundated with thirsty visitors. In no time, mother was serving home-made cakes and jams, then lunches, and soon offering beds for the night in the little cottage. Then racegoers began to drop in by the coachload on their way to a course several miles away.

World War I had been the first 'mechanized' war and many returning soldiers came home with a good army training as fitters, mechanics and drivers. They also had useful gratuities, and several set up their own village taxi or bus services. Fred Edgeworth, a red-haired Australian ex-

soldier, settled after the war in the Gloucestershire village of Ruscombe, and Don Hogg vividly recalls Fred's small red bus, christened the 'Meat Box', with kangaroos painted on each side and 14 wooden seats inside. Fred ran anything up to 17 trips a day, with no timetable and no tickets – he often let his hard-up regulars put their fares on the slate until payday. On cold days he was kept warm with cups of tea served by local women, and those of them who belonged to the village's new mail-order club rewarded him for collecting their parcels from the railway station with drinks at the inn. In 1928 Fred married one of his passengers and the villagers chaired him round the village, gave him handsome presents, filled him with beer and filled his bus with flowers for the bride.

By 1930 motorbuses had become comfortable saloons and were running regularly along the lanes from villages into market towns. The country bus dropped its passengers off in the market square and later delivered them and their parcel back to the heart of the village or, more often than not, dropped them off virtually on their own doorsteps. Passengers frequently travelled to town and back again in exactly the same bus, with the same driver and the same people. The bus willingly carried live chickens, goats, braces of ferreted rabbits, cottage cabbages and, on the return journey, goods from town – just like the old carrier's cart. Going by bus was the natural means of village transport and people became very fond of their country buses, some of which lived to a rattling good old age.

One such bus, or series of buses, was the 'Silver Queen'. The original, an old army ambulance, was bought in 1919 by Cecil Walling of Eastergate, Sussex, who converted it by fitting wooden seats for 14 passengers and covering its khaki coat with silver-grey paint. It was a friendly bus: its crews knew all the passengers by name and waited for regulars who were late. In winter they made sure that their elderly passengers could linger in the warmth of their cottages – the driver would stop at the gate and pip his horn for them. At Christmas villagers could flag the bus down to take their Christmas cards in its own GPO authorized postbox, or give their shopping lists to the crew, who would deliver the goods right to the cottage door on the return journey, or let people dump their shopping in the bus for delivery to their porches while they carried on buying up the town or went to the Picturedrome. 'Nobody ever left behind!' was the Silver Queen's slogan. It always waited for the last of its passengers after a show, and on one famous occasion it carried 63 people home after the pantomime, with many of the passengers travelling on its wings and footboards. The bus took the villagers to whist drives and darts matches; it carried the local football team to its away matches; it escorted tails of party-going cars on foggy nights, and the driver gave children an extra treat by accelerating over hump-backed bridges. Now, *that* was service!

～

Most commercial vehicles in the 1930s were petrol-driven, though there were still a few road steamwagons running on solid rubber tyres carrying very heavy loads. In 1895, England's first motor cars had been bound by the same 4 mph speed limit and red-flag rules as steam vehicles, but the flagman lost his job the following year and the limit was trebled. With the help of the Prince of Wales's purchase of a Daimler in 1900, private motoring became fashionable – and so speedy! The road dust billowed even more extravagantly; the hardcore of the period could not take the pace, cyclists complained about punctures, and horsemen swore at these dangerous new drivers. In 1909 *The Times*, giving

hints about night driving, warned that many horse drivers would be travelling with no lights on the crown of the road, the driver soundly asleep while the horse found its own way home. It had long been claimed that a farm horse should be able to carry home whisky and water; a water-drinking horse, that is to say, could safely transport a whisky-drinking man. Sadly, a car had no such instincts.

In the early years of the 20th century tar was used to seal a few macadamized roads, but country roads invariably remained stony dustbowls which had to be watered in dry weather to lay the dust, while minor lanes remained rutted cart-tracks. Wheeled vehicles took country roads as they found them. Local parish surveyors kept an eye on parish highways and local roadmen were still employed in

An early iron-wheeled motorbus belonging to the Aldershot & District Traction Company in Hampshire.

country areas during the 1930s. Each was a villager personally responsible for a certain length of road, keeping the verges in good order, cleaning out the grips and ditches, and taking considerable pride in 'his' length – feeling that he was directly answerable to the small community he served. Hard-working stone-breakers sat at the village crossroads with huge heaps of roadstone, endlessly hammering the stones into smaller pieces, and in many villages it was not until World War II that they were made redundant and the lane dust was finally laid by a skin of tarmac.

By 1924 there were more than half a million private motor cars in the country and at the outbreak of World War II there were two million (today there are ten times as many) but their owners remained middle and upper class, and cars were not common in rural areas. Maud Bridger remembers cycling with her fiancé in the early 1930s along the main London-to-Portsmouth road, where the traffic was so infrequent that the couple rode side by side with their arms draped over each other's shoulders. Ken Ainsworth, at the time a young stockman living near Leicester, would bike all the way to Wales for a day's outing, purely to enjoy the freedom of cycling, and thought nothing of doing the trip both ways in 24 hours, pausing only for a bite to eat before heading home again. After he married, Ken bought a tandem and the couple set off to visit his wife's family in Southampton. By the time they had pedalled to Newbury his wife's legs were tired so they put the machine on a train, got off again at Winchester and pedalled all the way to the port.

The middle-class motorists enjoyed 'touring' on the relatively uncrowded and rapidly improving roads, and they brought a little prosperity to some of the smaller coastal resorts and inland rural villages that had not been well served by the railways. But in September 1939, it was

the railways that transported 600,000 children from the cities into the safety of rural villages and farms, and by 1945 more than one and a half million evacuees would have been moved by rail. Yet between the two wars more than a thousand miles of railway, most of it rural branch lines, had been closed as uneconomical – closures which affected country life perhaps more than has been

OPPOSITE **In the 1920s motorcycles with sidecars became popular. Here an ingenious farmer finds a new way to take a calf to market.**

LEFT **Jigg Hill, a Sussex roadman in the 1920s. Local roadmen were a familiar and valued sight in every village, often much loved.**

ABOVE **A chauffeur-driven motor car in Berkshire, 1908.**

ABOVE RIGHT **Hikers joined the cycling tourists during the 1920s. Here a Sussex shepherd is showing the way.**

appreciated, helping to isolate villages again and leaving a yawning gap in transport which would be filled only after the war by the private car – that great enemy of village and countryside.

Before World War II, however, the railways brought commuters into the countryside. Trains made travelling to work so much easier and many urban workers moved to villages. But the scale of the exodus destroyed the very thing they dreamed about: as they pushed further out from the urban areas in search of the elusive village, they promptly turned it into an extension of the suburbs they had fled. Without commuter trains, the 'great escape', in full flow in the 1930s, would not have been possible. For the villagers, the railways were indeed a mixed blessing.

Part 2
Villagers

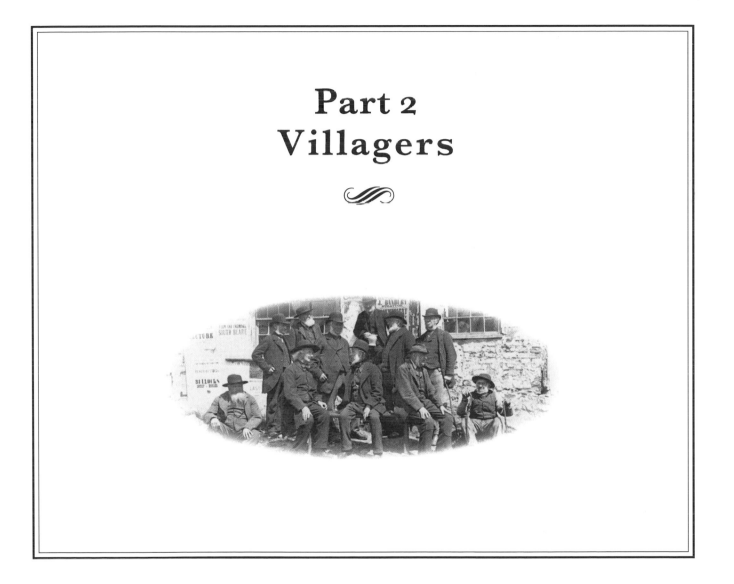

~~~

CHAPTER I

Squires

Long after the manorial system had been replaced by rural local councils towards the end of the 19th century, the paternalistic and conservative Victorian squire remained pivotal to the social structure of village life. Indeed, his influence locally remained strong right up to 1914 and in some areas up to 1939.

The term 'squire', a contraction of 'esquire', was applied to landowners, often (but not necessarily) lords of the manor, but almost invariably of old and respected families and members of the gentry, who lived on their land and were involved in county society, in contrast to the aristocratic absentee landowners who were more interested in the metropolis and its politics. Squires – and there were a couple of thousand of them in the country – were defined in 1850 as 'lesser gentry', owning between 1000 and 3000 acres and usually taking an active interest in how their land was farmed. Their landownership gave them local power but wealth was not the main criterion of their standing: the squirearchy was expected to have local roots, and 'old money' counted for much more than 'new' at least until later in the Victorian period.

By virtue of their landholdings, squires inevitably made impressions on local inhabitants, though no doubt the collective memory often exaggerated their characters and deeds. In my own valley, the squire (in the traditional sense of one who took a beneficent interest in the welfare of local people) appeared in the somewhat unlikely guise of the dynamic Yorkshire engineer Sir John Hawkshaw, builder of canals, bridges, railway stations, tunnels and London Underground's Inner Circle line. For a few years in his twenties, Sir John had been a mining engineer in Venezuela. As the major local landowner, Hawkshaw built a village school in the Italianate style – incorporating a stained-glass window in memory of his three children (Oliver, Maud and Mary) who had died in infancy – and plenty of stone estate cottages, mostly in pairs. He established a local brickyard, initially to make land-drainage tiles to improve the valley's damp farmland but later to make chimney pots, roofing tiles and bricks – a little village industry which would eventually send its produce all over the country. The family also built a reading room and, during the Boer War, a 25-yard indoor rifle range so that the valley's young men could improve their aim with a .22 in the evenings. It later became a working men's club with two full billiard tables and a venue for weekly whist drives and dances.

PREVIOUS PAGE **A group of village worthies in Stratton, Cornwall, 1887.**

By his deeds and caring, a benevolent squire could be a great blessing to the village, and he and his family could inspire considerable local loyalty and respect. Many squires were philanthropists with a genuine sense of duty to those less fortunate than themselves. The better squires would share family occasions with their employees, tenants and the rest of the village; their wives and daughters would entertain the village children and help with their education. Or they would donate practical gifts to the village's poor, build new cottages, help to maintain the fabric of the church, offer pensions and homes to long-term employees, lay on sports and games at holidays, share out the game bag at Christmas, and in countless other ways do their best to honour their responsibilities for the villagers' welfare.

Squire Coryton of Pentillie Castle, lord of the manor in the Cornish parish of Quethiock, was typical of this better type of squire. Originally from Devon, where they had settled in the 13th century, the Corytons acquired the manor of Trehunsey, in Quethiock, by marriages in the 17th and 18th centuries – Coryton men had the happy knack of marrying heiresses. Squire William Coryton (1847–1919) inherited the manor in 1891 from his unmarried uncle, Colonel Augustus Coryton, who lived with his sister at Pentillie Castle and was an excellent squire in the old tradition: lenient in his rent demands, but strict about good husbandry among his tenants. He was a staunch supporter of his local church and schools and took responsibility for several villages within his demesne. The *Cornish Times* for December 1884 captures well this sense of social duty.

During the week preceding Christmas the coverts were shot, resulting in an ample supply of pheasants and hares which were liberally distributed among the tenantry and others in the neighbourhood. Colonel Coryton's annual gifts in money and coals have been distributed to the poor of the neighbouring parishes. Miss Coryton's entertainment for the schoolchildren in Christmas week consisted of a capital Punch and Judy exhibition from Plymouth, followed by a substantial tea, concluding with an excellent imitation of waxworks by amateurs of the neighbourhood. Over 100 children were present.... The mechanics and labourers employed on the estate were, with their wives, entertained at dinner in the spacious Hall of Pentillie Castle, the party numbering 96, when full

Many squires, often lesser gentry but expected to be of 'good' old families, preferably with strong local roots, had a paternalistic sense of duty towards their villagers.

justice was done to the abundant supply of Christmas beef and pudding, and the real malt and hop ale brewed on the premises. A professional from Plymouth led off the appropriate songs after the various toasts, and also furnished the music for the dancing that followed.

On the marriage of his nephew, William, the Colonel gave all his employees a holiday and let them take sport by ferreting rabbits on the estate; he threw a party in the evening for nearly a hundred of the estate's servants and their friends at the castle, with music supplied by a quadrille band, while another hundred employees had a feast in the St Mellion schoolroom.

The Colonel died in his 82nd year and the *Western Morning News* was generous in its tribute to the 'warm-hearted owner of Pentillie Castle', describing him as a staunch churchman who 'held always that it was the duty of a landowner to contribute generously towards the maintenance of the church fabric'. Coryton also gave to various county charities and distributed private benefactions, ensuring that those who had served him well and faithfully were properly provided for in their old age. The squire's sister Charlotte (who died at the age of 79 in 1897) built a village school, held a Sunday school for many years, ran a night school, originated a Cherry Pie Feast at the castle for all the children from neighbouring parishes, and presented a handsome clock for St Mellion's church tower.

The old Colonel had farmed 1500 acres and made a policy of improving the land at every opportunity. The best squires were genuine countrymen with an inbred understanding of the land and a family tradition of caring for it, leaving it in good heart for future generations. They were firmly rooted in their environment and recognized that the land needed people to work on it, whether as employees or tenants. They took a personal interest in them, too, understanding that the land and the people were complementary and interdependent. They were often progressive farmers determined to put more heart into their land and to breed the very best livestock – and they encouraged their tenants to do likewise. A good squire was a generous employer, finding work on his farm in all seasons for local labourers. In connection with his field sports, several villagers found employment as gamekeepers and underkeepers, water bailiffs, beaters, woodsmen, kennel staff, stable hands and so on, while others were employed as domestic staff in the house and gardens.

In Shropshire, the Jordin family at Netherton rose to squirearchy during the 18th century by gradually acquiring property. Essentially farmers, by 1842 two Jordin brothers and their sons occupied by ownership or tenancy about half the farmland in the parish of Highley, having gradually squeezed out less successful neighbours. By 1851, brother William was listed in a directory as lord of the manor and principal landowner. By 1856 he was described under 'gentry' and was Highley's resident squire. He helped set up a village school for children of the 'labouring and manufacturing classes' and took the important step of renting land to the Highley Mining Company, which became a major employer in the parish. The Jordins were only 'minor' gentry – not a patch on the titled families in neighbouring parishes – but they were dominant in Highley and took the squirearchic role seriously. They owned a seven-bedroomed manor house, an old demesne farm, the mill, an inn, the blacksmith's shop, three or four other substantial houses and many of the cottages.

The true gentry – those of old families with long, known pedigrees – were genuinely respected in rural areas, almost regardless of personal character, but the industrial revolution had produced 'new' money and new self-styled

OPPOSITE **A beagle pack meets outside the manor house. Fox-hunting only became widely popular from the early 19th century and had a 'golden age' from about 1850 until World War I.**

A squire and his family on the beach.

of the village's empty 'big house': 'The labourers who never see their squire begin to look upon him as a sort of ogre, who exists merely to screw rents out of the land they till. Those who are dependent on land alone are often the men who do their duty best on their estates, and, poor though they may be, they are much beloved. But it is to be feared that in some parts of England men who are not suffering from the depression – rich tenants of country houses and the like – are apt to take a somewhat limited view of their duty towards their poorer neighbours.'

From the 1870s English agriculture suffered a depression that was to last 50 years. As the importance of agriculture in the national economy waned, the traditional squires gave way and sold their lands and their manor houses to town merchants, businessmen and property speculators who sought a weekend sporting life or socially prestigious homes. The old system of squirearchic responsibility that had knitted the rural community together gently crumbled. The sons of squires became farmers or shopkeepers or merchants or serving officers and only the memory of the squire's beneficent role together with concrete evidence in the shape of village buildings was left.

In 1919 Quethiock felt this wind of change very suddenly when the estate's 4200 acres were put up for auction as Squire William Coryton lay dying. The squire owned all but one farm in the parish and the auction lots included 29 farms, numerous smallholdings, the pub, the village school, the local post office, the smithy, the wheelwright's yard, the carpenter's shop, the mill, various village shops, the almshouses and many cottages and gardens. In fact most of the village was up for sale. At the time, most of the people were tenant farmers or husbandmen, with a few gamekeepers and woodsmen, served by the parson, schoolmaster, publican, shopkeepers, blacksmiths, carpenters, a miller, a mason, a wheelwright, a tailor and a

squires who, as the villagers saw it, had no right to such deference. They were not real countrymen and, however rich and powerful they might be, they did not have an innate understanding of the rhythms of the countryside or of the ways and sensibilities of the villagers.

As the 19th century progressed, the proportion of these new squires inevitably increased. They often managed to acquire titles and improved their images by building grand mansions filled with servants and surrounded by parkland, which separated them from the village in which the old squire had played such a day-to-day part. Arthur Gibbs wrote disparagingly of the absent squire and the sad sight shoemaker. With a population of about 430 in the whole parish and a mesh of connection by marriage, it was still a traditional, thriving, close-knit, self-sufficient rural community. Almost overnight the momentous sale destroyed the village's sense of security and continuity. Tenants of the better farms were easily outbid by the county council, cottagers lost their homes to covetous new owners, and workshops were snapped up by outsiders. For many it was a heart-rending experience as their roots, planted generations before, were suddenly loosened or even torn from the land that had sustained them.

The dying squire and his family had personally cared for them all. In the 1890s, when times were hard, he had allowed rent rebates to his tenant farmers; he had devised schemes to combat mass unemployment by undertaking major land-improvement schemes, including the building of many new dwellings, farmsteads, a new village post office, miles of stone-walling, new farm gates and wellheads: all over the parish there were signs of his close involvement in making life better for the villagers. Sometimes he helped on a more personal basis, ensuring, for example, that a young farm lad who had suffered a broken leg was given an apprenticeship to a good carpenter so that his future work would not involve miles of rough walking behind the plough, and he even built the lad a carpenter's shop at the end of the apprenticeship. The local council would never be so thoughtful!

✥

The aristocracy, still firmly at the top of the rural pyramid throughout the 19th century and well into the next, included those who owned huge acreages and controlled many rural lives but spent much of their time in the metropolis playing politics on a national scale. The first Earl of Iveagh, of the massive Elveden estate in Suffolk, was very much an aristocrat rather than a country squire. Born in Dublin in 1847 as Edward Cecil Guinness, the third son of a baronet, he employed 70 men in his game department alone and brought in another 100, dressed in red-collared white smocks and red-banded 'chummy' hats, to act as beaters on shooting days. His keepers wore bowler hats, brown suits and leather gaiters, and the head keeper co-ordinated this large army from the back of his pony with the aid of a German hunting horn: all for eight or nine guns at most! Each gun was attended by a loader and a cartridge boy, and the usual bag was expected to be at least a thousand pheasants a day. (The Duke of York, later King George V, somehow added a pig to his bag in 1899.) Harry Turner, the estate's head keeper for many years, well remembered the royal shooting days. Born in the 1870s, Harry had started his career at 16 by driving a cartload (literally) of cartridges for a visiting Maharajah. In later years poor Harry was deeply upset about the number of his young birds which were accidentally slaughtered during silage-making, but the second Lord Iveagh, while sympathizing, secretly smiled at the thought of all that extra protein for his cattle.

Another elderly employee on the Elveden estate was stableman Jim Jackson, who reached the age of 89 and was fortunate to do so – during the 1890s he had been bitten by a rabid dog. His life was saved because Guinness whisked him into the Pasteur Institute in Paris, where they were investigating hydrophobia. Two years later Guinness made a grateful endowment of £250,000 to the Lister Institute for Preventive Medicine in London – one of countless generous actions by this renowned philanthropist.

Many substantial estates and old-fashioned manor

RIGHT **A family living on the Sulham estate in Berkshire at the turn of the century.**

families still existed between the wars, carrying on much as their ancestors in employing local people on a large scale. Ruth Mott, for example, now in her seventies, still lives in the same Berkshire village cottage where she spent her childhood. Her father was gardener for the manor house and its lodge, the family of which took care of the village in the old way, giving estate workers lengths of cloth at Christmas, providing bowls of soup or milk puddings to women when they gave birth, teaching villagers to play the organ, rehearsing the church choir and arranging for the lads to learn the craft of copper-beating as a cottage industry.

At the age of 14 Ruth went into service. There were few other options. As work had to be within walking distance, nearly all the boys went into farmwork and the girls to the big houses. During Ruth's last term at school, prospective employers came to look over the leavers and Ruth was lucky enough to be chosen by the local manor house. Two days after the end of term, her father put her case into a wheelbarrow and off they went. She lived in, of course, staying in every evening unless the mistress gave her permission to attend a village dance, with half a day off a week and an afternoon every second Sunday to visit her family. Her working day began at 6.15 in the morning and did not finish until 9.30 at night, with only a short afternoon break. Gradually climbing the ranks from kitchenmaid, Ruth eventually became a cook in charge of two dozen staff.

Miss Buckingham, born at the turn of the century, was another gardener's daughter. Her father was head gardener on a big estate, in charge of a team of ten caring for conservatory carnations, vineries, peach-houses, palm trees in a green-glassed conservatory alive with twittering birds and fountains, extensive kitchen gardens, pleasure gardens and wild gardens surrounding an old manor house. The

grandson of the dowager viscountess who lived in the house recalls Miss Buckingham's father strutting about in his bowler hat: 'As far as I can remember, I never saw him use a spade!' The present viscount, now living two counties away, remembers the beautiful gardens vividly and recalls riding out with his grandmother in a black landau with splendid black horses and a coachman and footman in full livery – though some locals say she also drove a team of white mules and at least one villager claims to have seen the ghost of a white mule at the ford below the mansion. The coal-black horses were sent across the Channel to 'do their bit for England' during the Great War: one was killed in action, the other was injured by shrapnel and brought home to be buried in the rickyard along with the rest of the estate's beloved ponies, pets and housecows.

Before 1914 the dowager employed a butler, a housekeeper, a lady's maid, two housemaids, three in the pantry, three more in the kitchen, and a secretary-cum-companion. Eleven men were employed in the gardens and two more in the stables, many living in surrounding cottages. Charlie Wakeford looked after seven Jersey cows and Polly the pony, whose trap took staff to the town and

who also mowed the mansion's lawns, wearing special shoes. There were always four pigs for killing three times a year; ducks and chickens, and a lake full of trout – everything in fact the house needed to be self-sufficient. The pigs were killed by the village butcher, who kept two for his own expenses; one of the others was for the house and one to be shared among the staff. Sides of bacon were smoked, in an enormous inglenook in the old farmhouse down the lane. The estate's water was pumped up from streams and springs to an enormous tank on the hill, and the constant background muttering of pumps could be heard all over the valley.

In the dowager's time, the house was always full of guests. She loved to entertain and the wide-eyed servants looked after several Scandinavian kings, the young Winston Churchill, and the Kaiser – who enjoyed a game of indoor tennis. Charlie Wakeford, the cowman, living in a little stone cottage nearby, saved the lives of a houseful of such fine guests after a ball on Bonfire Night in 1902. Waking in the early hours of the morning to attend his invalid wife he saw that the big house was on fire, its occupants apparently oblivious of the fact. It took the fire brigade several hours to arrive on that very foggy night (a man with a lamp walking ahead of the horses to guide them) and much of the house was destroyed.

Documents concerning the sale of the estate in 1896 reveal a great deal about the cottagers and traders who lived within its borders. The main mansion had stables, coach houses, outhouses, yards, farmsteads, lawns, gardens, shrubberies, pleasure grounds, gardeners' cottages and bothies (where the unmarried men lived), an acre of 'several sheets of water', a stream, orchards, paddocks, closes and plantations. Along the lane below the mansion was a house once known as the Woodcutter Beerhouse, a parcel of glebeland, a piece of land formerly the site of a

LEFT **Mrs Lewis of Milland, Sussex, who lived in the estate's Laundry Cottage and had used many of the same methods and equipment for half a century when the laundry finally closed down in 1953.**

shoemaker's shop and several cottages, each tenant and previous tenants carefully named and described. Sold for less than £13,000, the whole estate went to a man living in a house called 'Bellvue' in Reigate – hardly the abode of a traditional squire!

～ﾟ∞ﾟ～

By virtue of their wealth some landowners could not resist treating the village as their private toy. Many magnanimously improved and rebuilt their villages over several decades or generations, but others knocked down entire communities at one blow because their view was interrupted and a few mighty landowners built brand-new villages from scratch – carefully planned entities in which all the buildings were erected on a new site. These privately built villages are betrayed now by their uniformity of age and the sense of an overall designer, even in cases where each cottage was deliberately designed to be different.

Most model villages were created by individuals wishing to give workers better homes, to shift an obstruction from a landscape view, or as self-indulgent architectural exercises. Inevitably, the majority of these 'visionaries' were substantial rural landowners – often dukes – though some were wealthy industrialists. Occasionally the new villages were communities based on religious or political beliefs, but only rarely were they conceived and built by villagers.

New rural villages were still being built in the mid 19th century. Sindelsham Green, Dorset, for example, was built at the gates of Bearwood by its owners, the Walter family, who gave their village an inn as well as almshouses, a school and a church. Several villages of this period, however, were in the fashionable 'picturesque' style, with the emphasis on 'cottages' and a harmonious mixture of styles along winding streets (in contrast to the linear, uniform estate villages). They were picture-postcard constructions which appealed more to the Victorian romantic pastoral ideal than the practical realities of rural life – places like the Suffolk village of Somerleyton, and the Duke of Devonshire's Chatsworth estate village of Edensor.

It was not only rural landowners who built villages. Paternalistic employers intent on improving industrial housing built self-contained village communities for their workers in rural areas. Saltaire, conceived in 1849 by the Yorkshire woolmill magnate Titus Salt, was built around Salt's new mohair mill north of Bradford, and so designed that the size of each house varied according to the status of the occupants. With nearly 800 dwellings, together with almshouses, churches, chapels, public baths, steam laundry, hospital, school, and park with bandstand, Saltaire was more a town than a village.

In the 1890s Lord Leverhulme created his famous Port Sunlight in Cheshire and the estate village of Thornton Hough nearby. In 1901 chocolate king Joseph Rowntree built his village of New Earswick outside York, with 500 cottages, its own village hall and school and an enormous green. Chocolate seemed to generate villages: Amos Hexton, the owner of a cocoa factory, built Hextonville for his workers, and the Cadbury family's Bournville was another cocoa village, built in 1895.

Cadbury, Rowntree and Hexton were Quakers and several Quaker industrialists put their religious beliefs into practice by building villages. An early example is Street in Somerset: it had a population of about 800 in 1825 when C. & J. Clark founded their shoe-making business there, initially based on cottage industry. By 1861 its population was 1900, and more than double that in 1901.

OPPOSITE **Great Tew, Oxfordshire, in 1938. Designed by J. C. Loudon in 1808 as part of an agricultural improvement scheme, it is typical of villages designed and maintained as a whole unit by some of the major landowners and improvers of the 18th and 19th centuries.**

Then there were religious and political movements intent on founding colonies for their adherents. The most prominent of these community-builders were the Moravian Brethren, whose communal settlements centred on chapel and school; they had all they needed to be self-sufficient including bakeries, shops, weaving sheds and graveyards. The localized Society of Dependents, known as the Cokelers (they preferred cocoa to alcohol), established co-operative shops – partly, it seems, to ensure that their members could attend weekday services – and the Sussex village of Loxwood, near the Surrey border, has a whole row of shops built by its Cokelers in the 19th century.

Model village-building continued during the 20th century. Ardeley in Hertfordshire, for example, was built in 1917–18 by the local lord of the manor; and Whiteley Village in Surrey was founded in 1911 as a memorial to the immensely wealthy William Whiteley, owner of the famous store in London's Bayswater. World War I really brought to an end the long reign of wealthy landed gentry, and badly dented the substantial 19th-century industrial families too, though F. H. Crittall built a village for his windowmakers in the late 1920s at Silver End in Essex and Lord Rothschild, as late as 1965, rebuilt the village of Rushbrook, near Bury St Edmunds, Suffolk, for his tenants. But many of the old families were taxed half to death by estate duties after World War I and could hardly afford to maintain their own homes, let alone build whole villages.

Real villages – homes for rural workers – are rarely now the responsibility of benevolent private landowners. Housing and welfare have been taken over by local authorities and public bodies. Local government came to the countryside when county councils were created in 1888 (50 years later than urban local authorities), but the new bodies were dominated by the country's gentry and it was many years before the 'old guard' of nobility and squires ceded their former roles. Indeed, it was not until World War I that villagers began to reject the view that their 'betters' knew best, though there was a strong tendency for agricultural workers to vote for the 'yaller' rather than the blue (Liberal rather than Tory). As Arthur Gibbs noted in the late 1890s, nine out of ten villagers were Radicals at heart, and Gibbs greatly admired his local village politician, with whom he spent many hours chatting in his snug hamlet cottage over a cup of tea. 'Common sense he has to a remarkable degree, and a good deal more knowledge than most people give him credit for,' he declared.

On one memorable occasion, Gibbs found himself canvassing at Northleach for his Unionist member, who had just been unseated from his three-vote majority by a recount. The innocent Gibbs was invited to chair a meeting in the town and discovered that he was facing 'two hundred red-hot Radicals, with only one other speaker besides myself to keep the ball a-rolling'. Young Gibbs was a nervous speaker who easily lost the thread of his argument if interrupted – which he frequently was, of course – and the din became so great that his voice could not possibly be heard until he had the bright idea of *singing*! The audience then immediately stopped their heckling to listen. 'When, as a final climax, I finished up with a prolonged B flat – a very loud and long note, which sounded to me something between a "view holloa" and the whistle of a penny steamboat, but which came in nicely as a sort of *pièce de résistance*, fairly astonishing "Hodge" – their enthusiasm knew no bounds. They cheered and cheered again. Hand shaking went on all around, whilst the biggest Radical of the lot stood up and shouted, "You be a little Liberal, I know!" .'

OPPOSITE

Electioneering in the village of East Tisted, Hampshire, in the 1880s.

In 1894 another Local Government Act established urban and rural district councils and, within the rural districts, civil parish councils as the grassroots of local administration in rural communities with populations of more than 300. The Act finally separated the functions of the ecclesiastical parish from the civil parish.

Initially, the parish councils were expected to revive self-government in the villages and at the same time to counterbalance the ambitions of its old rulers, the squire and the parson. They were supposed to become village parliaments, with smallholders and craftsmen as their members, but they were given very little real power and even less money and they simply did not have the muscle to put the old duo in their place. In fact, more often than not, the squire or the parson became chairman of the parish council and the more substantial local farmers became members with the strength to block any 'undesirable' reforms put forward by members with less status.

Whatever the legislature, social attitudes do not change overnight – especially in villages. The old rural class system merely adapted itself to comply with the new laws. Major landowners and squires naturally dominated the county councils while the parsons, farmers and traders took control of both district and parish councils. While the majority of villagers accepted this as quite right and proper, the old guard sincerely believed that they had a moral obligation to continue in their governing roles and were best suited for the job anyway.

The new system, however, finally spelled the end of the old village in that it challenged its whole social structure based on the squirearchy. The old order was weakened and its often beneficial role undermined, although even a century later there are faint traces of it in some rural areas. But the whole concept of the village as a social unit responsible for its own weaker members had been thoroughly shaken by the Local Government Acts and would be further shattered in due course by the increasing intrusion of outside agencies, middle-class urban settlers and, ultimately, the welfare state which finally supplanted the squire-and-parson role towards villagers.

CHAPTER 2

Farmers

Beneath the controlling aristocrats and landed gentry in 1850, in social terms, were yeoman farmers, owning from a hundred to a thousand acres which they actively farmed themselves. Farming was in their blood. Some came from a long line of yeoman families stretching back to the Middle Ages and in Victorian times many were prosperous. But their ranks were swelled by a new class of landowner with no understanding of the land – tradesmen and manufacturers who saw country land-ownership as a step up the social ladder.

The yeoman was less than a gentleman but had higher social standing than a tradesman and the majority of working tenant farmers. The typical yeoman – in fact as well as in nostalgic folk memory – was sturdy, down-to-earth, hardworking, ruddy-faced, thrifty, often illiterate and a stalwart of village life, and was likely to run the village if there was no resident squire. Eventually, and inevitably, some yeomen became true squires and some earned themselves titles. Arthur Gibbs called them 'yeoman princes', men who not only possessed their own freeholds but farmed an additional thousand acres or more, like the Garne family of Aldsworth, Gloucestershire, who were celebrated breeders of Shorthorn cattle and Cotswold sheep.

Robert Garne, a lifelong bachelor until his death at 75 in 1900, inherited his father's 1100-acre farm in 1857 and was a big, strong, dominant man who 'ruled' the village and was both respected and feared over a wide area. He was looked after by a faithful housekeeper, Miss Miller, and his farm was under the care of foreman Blake, who lived a quarter of a mile away from Garne's house 600 feet up on the cold, bleak limestone hills. First thing every morning, Garne would open his bedroom window wide and bawl his orders for the day across the fields to Blake's distant home.

Robert Garne had a ruthless commercial streak – he was as much a shrewd businessman as an expert sheep-breeder – which enabled him to acquire much property and make his fortune in spite of the agricultural depression of the last quarter of the century. When he died, Garne left what today would be the equivalent of more than £2 million and his will carefully distributed it to various relatives: not a penny was left, however, to any of his employees who had helped him build his fortune.

George Dew described several Oxfordshire farmers, a group whom he apparently disliked in general and whom, as members of the Board of Guardians, he deemed as

A gentleman farmer:
William Hales
(1796–1867) of
Shortwood House
in Lamport,
Northamptonshire.
He was the father of
four sons and four
daughters.

inappropriately severe. Among the Board was one Sir Henry Dashwood, Bart., of Kirtlington Park, at whose insistence 72-year-old Hannah Cato, still actively working as an agricultural labourer, was denied relief because her sons had been poaching on his land. Sir Henry, though standing as a Liberal, was, said Dew, far from being liberal and held 'game almost as tightly as gold'. Dew was particularly shocked at Dashwood's severity to Hannah, which persisted even though she had broken her arm and could no longer earn her paltry four shillings a week.

Dashwood, a 'corpulent, good-looking man, rather swarthy in complexion, and lately slightly deaf', was a magistrate and employed 55 agricultural workers on his home farm in 1871, and also a score of domestic staff and a governess. His brother lived in the same mansion and farmed a separate 1175 acres, employing another 52 labourers. James Cheesman, a prosperous yeoman farmer at Caldecote, had employed 18 men, nine boys and four women on his 467 acres in 1871; ten years later he had increased the acreage to 644 but reduced his employees to 23 (a sign of mechanization) and also employed a governess and three domestic servants.

Mechanization helped a very different farmer, William Padbury King at Rectory Farm, where he employed only ten men and six boys on his 311 acres. King bought a new reaping machine in 1870 for nearly £30 and claimed that it saved him four shillings an acre in cutting his corn as it could do the work of 16 men. Unmarried at 37 and living with his widowed mother and a sister, King was a churchwarden for many years.

Different again was Henry Coldicott, who in 1870 faced charges for selling hides off his farm though they were known to be infected with foot-and-mouth disease. Coldicott was a man with a 'vile unmanageable temper' who swore violently after the magistrates' hearing. 'With all his money and haughtiness,' commented Dew, 'I believe him to be one of the most inexorable tyrants, to any person who dare to slightly thwart him, that this County affords.' Nor did Dew like farmer William Hore, whose sisters complained about the 'nuisance' of a pigsty on Dew's premises next to theirs. 'Of all the arrogant fools.... He hardly knew how to be civil, and he appeared to lack every quality which distinguishes a gentleman.... I found him a near Infidel. He is the best educated reprobate in the neighbourhood.'

By the 1850s, the larger tenants and landowners had achieved huge increases in productivity from land and livestock, and agriculture was prosperous – for the landowner and the large tenant farmer, that is. Yeomen were beginning to style themselves gentlemen and the more successful tenant farmers became even more successful capitalists and businessmen, growing profits as well as crops. Meanwhile, the less ambitious or less fortunate yeomen and traditional smallholders were gradually squeezed off the land and either looked for waged farmwork or drifted reluctantly into the towns in search of new opportunities.

The gap between farmer and worker was made that much greater by this thinning of the ranks of the intermediate group. The labourers, who were usually highly skilled husbandmen, became relatively poorer, badly fed and badly housed as the new rural middle class came into its own. Farmers and their families no longer shared the workers' labour and they no longer shared their table or their home with their men: they were no longer fellow workers but, decidedly, masters – a common term applied to them by all farmworkers, in some areas right up to World War II.

The early Victorian master did not rate literacy highly; he had little culture and no knowledge of national or international affairs, but he did know his land and passed on his farming skills to the next generation, who learned by practical experience rather than from college textbooks. The tenants of medium-sized farms tended to vote as the squire suggested and were conservative by nature, content enough with the old ways of simple living, sharing the table with the farm's workers and relaxing with the family in the evening, the master no doubt smoking a clay pipe and nursing a mug of ale.

The Chalcraft family ready for tennis, a fashionable pastime for middle-class farmers of the period, many of whom turned their paddocks into tennis courts.

These genteel families began to exclude their workers from the farmhouse, no longer sharing the table, and forcing them to live in the village instead. They enjoyed balls and tea-parties, musical evenings, weekend house-parties, charades, croquet, tennis and archery, and neglected the traditional Michaelmas feasts for the workforce which Cotswold labourer John Brown recalled from the 1840s when ''twere all mirth and jollity'. Brown, looking back when he was in his late seventies, said: 'There was four feasts in the year for us folk. First of all there was the sowers' feast – that would be about the end of April; then came the sheep-shearers' feast – there'd be about fifteen of us as would sit down after sheep-shearing, and we'd be singing best part of the night, and plenty to eat and drink; next came the feast for the reapers, when the corn was cut about August; and, last of all, the harvest home in September. Ah! those were good times fifty years ago.'

By the 1870s, the old harvest festivities had virtually disappeared into folk memory over most of the country, with only their shadows lingering in the subdued, orderly, organized harvest festival which the Victorians had firmly drawn inside the church. No more decorated harvest wagons, no more Michaelmas goose and ginger wine, no more speeches and loyal toasts and drawing on pipes filled with freely offered shag, no more riotous singing and dancing after the feast – no more shared celebration as a richly deserved reward for a year's hard work in the fields and reforging the links between farmers and workers. No more Plough Monday, dragging the decorated plough around the village to collect money, indulging in sports and eating gingerbread and Christmas cake at every farm in the parish. Farmers had become too distant for all of that.

The habit of eating in the friendly kitchen with the farmhands had already become unusual by the 1850s. The

Thomas Woodman's farm staff at Littlecote, Stewkley, Buckinghamshire, c. 1870.

The old farmhouse had been home to an extended household including domestic and farm servants, all fed and bedded within it. The most used room was the large 'houseplace', which combined kitchen and living-room and was essentially a place for cooking, eating, keeping warm and chatting. As the Victorian era progressed, the lifestyle and homes of more substantial farm households began to reflect their social ambitions. Farmers decided that their womenfolk should no longer demean themselves by any involvement in the farm, not even in dairywork and the poultry yard which had always been their provinces. Wives began to see themselves as household managers rather than farm helpers, and their daughters were encouraged to become 'accomplished', learning to play the piano and follow ladylike pursuits such as needlework, art and dancing.

family's living-room was now a large Victorian parlour, its chairs scratchily stuffed with horsehair, its planked floor covered with linoleum or canvas or the daughters' hand-stitched carpets and hearth-rugs, a couple of family portraits on the walls, a Bible on a side-table and perhaps a boardgame to prove that they had some idle hours. The more advanced turned their big open fireplaces into coal-burning grates within a side-oven rather than cooking over an open fire with a kettle hanging on the hook and meat roasting on a spit.

The home of John Waine provides one such example. A maltster and brewer who bought a small farmhouse in the early 1850s, Waine converted it by giving it a Georgian façade and sash windows. He added a large cellar for his beer barrels and an extensive malthouse. Fifty years later the house was bought by a well-off farmer who added a new wing and a conservatory, resited the front door, put in a fine oak staircase, installed indoor sanitation and a bathroom and, unusually for the time, solid-fuel central heating and a private acetylene-gas plant for lighting. He built splendid stables with tackroom and coach house and converted the old rickyard into a walled glass peach-house, a fruit garden, orchard and tennis court (all the rage with turn-of-the-century farming families). He employed a gardener and a chauffeur for his new car and, in due course, acquired the first telephone in the village.

Many old-style yeoman squires in more remote regions continued their traditional farming life and were of the type which often springs to mind at the mention of the word 'squire': red of face, rough in manner, hearty, hunting-crazy, bucolic, loud-laughing and fond of bawdy jokes. They were down-to-earth men, know-where-you-stand men, no-nonsense men; they worked hard and played hard, and were often well respected though not necessarily loved by their workers.

British agriculture reached a peak of prosperity in about 1870, the golden age of 'high farming'. Farm sizes had grown considerably by amalgamation, while smaller squires gave way to larger landowners and often their small manor houses became the homes of tenant farmers. It was a time of optimism for most in the countryside, but it did not last.

With the application of free trade from the 1870s, the continuing high demand for food in urban areas was met increasingly not by home-grown produce but by importing food from the very countries to which many young villagers had fled in difficult times. Grain and frozen meat poured in from the American continent and Australasia, to the delight of the consumer but with disastrous effect on English farmers. The position of Britain's farmers was further undermined by a series of appallingly wet years in the late 1870s, which left crops unharvestable and livestock disease widespread. It seemed that nature, as well as free trade, had conspired against the English farmer.

Those farmers who had aspired to gentility felt the crash most keenly. The more socially pretentious among them found themselves in deep trouble: they defaulted on their rents, went bankrupt, moved to smaller farms or left farming altogether. They cut their workforces to the minimum and thousands of labourers left the land for good.

But some were to gain from their neighbours' misfortune. The farmers of Wales and south-west England, used to harder conditions, were only too willing to step into vacated farms and to reintroduce the type of farming that those departed 'improvers' had considered beneath them. These old-fashioned farmers kept calves in the parlour and pigs in the sitting-room; they stacked manure in the dining-room, and the old kitchen again became the heart of the farmhouse. The house, often by then an old manor

Milk churns on their way from farm to railway station in the 1920s. The combination of rail transport and chilling techniques greatly widened the dairy farmers' markets.

house, became the centre of a working farm once again, with the farm buildings clustered comfortably around it, just as they always had been in the traditional farmstead.

During the second phase of the great agricultural depression in the 1890s, more than 2 million acres of arable land became little better than weeds and rough grazing with no increase in livestock to graze it. The south of England was by far the worst hit and country lanes echoed dully to the shuffling feet of tramps and vagrants, of both sexes, begging by day, calling in at the local workhouse for supper, bed and breakfast, then breaking a hundredweight of road-mending stones in payment before roaming the lanes again. Those who could find farm work were as badly paid and badly fed as before, and still as dependent on charity. This situation persisted until the outbreak of war in 1914 when farming was briefly rescued by the increased demand for home-produced food.

After the war, farming experienced yet another depression in the 1920s and 1930s, hitting hardest the new postwar farmers, many of them ex-servicemen starting a new life after the horrors of the trenches. With no capital to tide them through, they lost everything. Many of the better-cushioned among them resorted to 'dog-and-stick' farming by reducing to a minimum their equipment, employees and outgoings and simply grazing store cattle on uncultivated arable land. Farm rents tumbled but few could take advantage of them. Workers' wages were cut and, yet again, many left the land. Farm walls and hedges were neglected; cottages fell into disrepair and tumbled into heaps of rubble.

For some, the series of depressions gave impetus for a new, successful life. In 1880, George Garne saw what was coming and sold his entire farm and stock in order to take over a country brewery at Burford in Oxfordshire. He became a successful brewer, maltster and hop merchant, and his son, Willy, was still working a full day in the family brewery's office at the age of 91.

In the 1920s, several shattered farmers threw away their pride, got themselves old vans and set up milk rounds that became the foundations of substantial dairies. Others simply left the land forever, though some would come back after World War II when there were cheap farms and estates going begging. By then the land and agriculture would have changed: the tractor would have displaced the horse, resulting in far fewer jobs on the land. There would be no more singing in the fields.

The change from horses to tractors was cautious in many places, in spite of government incentives. Here, both types of horsepower are at work in the same field.

CHAPTER 3

Church and Chapel

The age-old partnership and rivalry between the parson and the local landowner persisted throughout the 19th century. The parson was involved in the practical as well as spiritual welfare of the villagers, especially in caring for the poor, the sick and the aged, sharing this role with the squire to a degree that depended on the character of both. Sometimes the Victorian squire was also the parson, or 'squarson', so that the village was dominated by one man without the counterbalance that had helped parson and squire to control each other over the centuries.

Parsons and poverty were always linked, partly through the priest's pastoral duty in caring for the poor and partly because of his own pressing needs for an income to carry out that duty effectively and also to live on himself. Whatever the Bible taught about treasure on earth, it was money (or the lack of it) which necessarily took up much of the parson's time and thoughts, and he spent much ingenuity devising schemes to increase it. In earlier times some took a cut from the smugglers who used the churchyard tombs as hiding places for contraband. In the 19th century, parsons developed sidelines in minor trades; some took in pupils; some grew and sold crops from the glebeland or even the churchyard, while others printed and sold their sermons to other parsons.

While many parsons had a genuine interest in improving social conditions, it seems that some were more intent on improving their own status than that of the poor. George Dew, as the local Relieving Officer, frequently castigated the five parsons on his Board of Guardians for their lack of charity, complaining that while many of them had large incomes from the Church, part of which was intended for relieving the poor, 'when they have a voice in the distribution of Parochial Relief the chances on the side of human nature are that they will relieve themselves at the expense of the Ratepayer.' Indeed, he said, very often the clergymen were 'relieved of giving anything in kind, excepting his spiritual ministrations; and they themselves know how valuable a copious supply of relief is in saving their own pockets.' Dew was particularly incensed at the attitude of the Rev. William John Dry, vicar of Weston Green, Oxfordshire, who was chairman of the Board of Guardians at Bicester's workhouse and popularly known as 'the Weston Devil'. 'For some twelve months,' wrote Dew of the Rev. Dry, 'he had been cutting off every atom of outdoor relief which it was possible to do; and I can most

truthfully assert that I do not think any Union in the Kingdom can boast of a district in which less relief in proportion to the destitution is given .... It has been driven to the extreme, and all this under the guidance and direction of a clergyman of the Established Church, whose duty specially it is to relieve the destitute and minister both spiritually and bodily to their necessities.'

Dew thought as little of most parsons as he did of most farmers. The fiery curate at Souldern, Dr J. E. W. Rotton, was accused of assaulting the stonemason's wife, so alarming her that she 'had to lie in bed and have medical attendance several days afterwards', though he had only lifted his hand as if to strike and the case was dismissed. Rotton was known as a violent man and his parish disliked him even more when he began levelling all the graves, locking the churchyard gates, and reading extracts from Acts of Parliament during his sermons. He also demolished the church's old gallery. His rector, old Dr Stephenson, was by then very feeble and in despair over his own family: his wife was a peculiar woman whom nobody in the village ever saw, their son had fathered at least one illegitimate child by a maid at the rectory, and one of the Stephenson daughters married but never bothered to live with her husband. Or so village gossip went.

Some parsons were comfortable enough – the rector of Somerton was offered £4000 for his living in 1874 but held out for more – but in many places stipends were so laughably small that the clergy gathered themselves more than one benefice in order to survive under the system known as 'pluralism'. These pluralist parsons (most villagers called them all parsons, whether rector, vicar or curate), hampered by impassable rural lanes between their livings, usually found themselves overstretched and often virtual strangers in their own parishes. A rather chaotic system of pluralism, absenteeism and deputizing persisted

LEFT **John Whitmore Black, rector of Launcells, Cornwall, in Stratton's main street, c. 1900. He had been appointed to the living in 1873.**

throughout most of the 19th century as a consequence.

The parson's many outgoings included payment of his parish clerk's wages. The clerk, a layman, was appointed by the parson and his duties included keeping church records and accounts, ensuring the congregation behaved itself, making the lead responses, reading the epistles and lessons, and ringing the church bell to summon worshippers to services. He conducted the hymn-singing, too, with illiterates repeating each line after him and singing along to the music of his pitch-pipe or the village's band of fiddles and woodwinds or, later, the clerk's efforts on the barrel-organ, pipe-organ or harmonium.

Some clerks were thorough reprobates. In 1863, one

William Arnold, a parish clerk at Bradford Abbas, Dorset.

Henry West was deposed as parish clerk for misconduct and sent to prison for rioting. In 1874, as a journeyman carpenter, he was indicted for building houses on the highway: he was compelled to demolish them and some of his property was seized. In revenge, a week later, he demolished the hedges and garden wall of a cottage belonging to the Oxford college which had indicted him, claiming that *they* were encroaching on the highway. He was given three weeks' hard labour for malicious damage.

Most parish clerks, however, were thoroughly worthy people. The majority were ordinary farm labourers (including women) and they were genuine villagers. Unlike the semi-itinerant parson, the clerk was always there, and indeed the village often held him in higher esteem than the unfamiliar parson. The clerk became the village uncle: he gave away fatherless brides and was godfather to numerous children. But the old-fashioned clerk gave way to the Victorian verger, who in turn, by the 1920s, was also disappearing along with the old sexton whose family had been grave-diggers for several generations.

The churchwarden had already lost much of his former status as the village's lay representative keeping an eye on the fabric of the church and its treasures, and on the parson as well, making sure he carried out his duties to the village's satisfaction. Although his once extensive financial powers and earlier civil duties had been divested, the churchwarden (often a yeoman farmer) remained a much respected member of the community and might be effectively the village headman if there was no resident vicar or squire.

George Dew was, together with his many other duties in the village, both churchwarden and clerk to the civil parish council, posts he held until 1928 (the year of his death), when at the age of 82 he proudly noted in his diary that he had attended his 32nd parish council audit. In contrast, Arthur Gibbs in the early 1890s had mistakenly accepted the post of churchwarden when he was only 24 and did not recommend it at all, complaining, 'You become a sort of acting aide-de-camp to the parson, liable to be called out on duty at a moment's notice.' His advice to young men was that they might, with some advantage to others and with credit to themselves, take on the office of parish councillor, Poor Law guardian, 'Inspector of Lunatic Asylums, High Sheriff, or even Public Hangman; but save, oh, save us from being churchwardens! To be obliged to attend those terrible institutions called "vestry meetings" and to receive each year an examination paper from the archdeacon of the diocese propounding such questions as, "Do you attend church regularly? If not, why not?" etc, etc, is the natural destiny of the churchwarden, and is more than human nature can stand.'

The vestry, a room attached to the church where vestments and ornaments are kept, was the customary meeting-place for the body of parishioners who elected the churchwardens and supervised the collection of funds for repairs to the church. These open vestry meetings also dealt with a wide range of non-church matters and were the predecessors in that respect of today's civil parish councils, giving villagers a say in local affairs so that they felt they had an influence on what happened in their own village. In the 1890s, however, the new civil parish councils usurped the vestry's administration of the Poor Law and in 1919 an Enabling Act created parochial church councils to take over the vestry meeting's ecclesiastical responsibilities.

There was no such person as a typical 19th-century parson, of course, but there were plenty of interesting characters. The vicar of Ablington, Gloucestershire, for example, was one of the few Tories of the old school who ruled his parish with a rod of iron and whose word was law. Loved and respected by most of his parish (one old man greatly admired him for being 'so scratchy after souls'), he seldom left the village except for his annual holiday, but he knew and related all the latest gossip from Belgravia. He had property in Somerset but his heart remained in his adopted village, where he ruled for more than a quarter of a century. Some parsons seemed to go on forever – the Rev. W. W. Wingfield was vicar of Guval, Cornwall, for nearly 74 years and was still preaching sermons at the age of 94 during World War I.

The rural church often attracted eccentrics, such as

A Sussex grave-digger at work in the 1920s.

Dunsfold Old Bells. 1587 1625 1649

The old church bells at Dunsfold, Surrey, dated 1587, 1625 and 1649.

nominal rates as allotments so that farmworkers could grow produce for cottage and market. Inevitably some such parsons came into conflict with farmers, indirectly by giving the workers 'ideas' or deliberately by fighting for higher wages for them. Parson Girdlestone of Halberton, Devon, openly voiced his anger at low agricultural wages in the 1860s and actively encouraged men to find better work elsewhere; he even found jobs for them in other counties and assisted them with transport there. His actions, involving several hundred men, created a local labour shortage which effectively forced the farmers to offer higher wages.

Life in a modern vicarage in 1847 featured a daily bath in a tin tub, a house lit by candles and oil-lamps, a cottage widow helping with the baking, and poultry in the yard. The parson's standard of living benefited from the rapid improvement in agricultural techniques, which increased the value of his tithes and glebelands (though he had long since ceased to labour on his own land), and his status grew with his income. Like the tenant farmers, many Victorian parsons became quite prosperous and began to climb the social ladder, extending or rebuilding their parsonages just as the farmers improved their farmhouses. In Highley, Shropshire, for example, the incumbent until 1843 had been Samuel Burrows who, like his predecessors, was upper middle class and university educated though, unlike them, he lived in the village and employed local servants. His vicarage was one of the two 'big houses' (the other was that of the squire) and continued to be so under his successor, Samuel du Pre, who was the parson there until the 1880s. The directories for 1870 show du Pre and the squire as the chief landowners.

parson Conybeare of Barrington, Cambridgeshire, who was a Greek scholar and inventor with a sense of humour – adding a front seat to his bicycle, he perched his wife on it and rode about the village after dark using a gunpowder flash to bombard children with sweets. Others were more serious and became involved with education, partly from their dutiful concern for the poor but also as a means of improving their income. Some, like Charles Kingsley (1819–75), were practising Christian Socialists and carried their concern much further, pressing for better rural cottages, better medical services, better sanitation (the earth closet was invented by a vicar), establishing working men's clubs and renting out their own glebelands at

The mid-Victorian country parson was generally happy enough to live a simple quiet life, busying about his parish's little businesses, presiding over predictable services, preaching bland sermons in contrast to the fire-belly chapel preachers, arranging penny readings, teaching RI (Religious Instruction) in the schoolroom, holding tea-parties, organizing magic-lantern shows and evening lectures, and perhaps concerts and glee classes. But as the Victorian era wore on, the link between parson and parishioner grew weaker and more impersonal. There were even a few 19th century parsons who did their best to keep parishioners *out* of the church, luring them away with sixpenny bribes or wine at the rectory instead of the bother of church services. A certain vicar in Cornwall in the 1870s decided that the neighbouring incumbent could also look after his parish for him while he strolled about his garden next to the church, smoking and deigning to gossip with his own parishioners as they left the service. What a contrast to some of the colourful characters who forced their flock into church, even driving them out of the inns with a whip!

The later Victorian parsons were often shabbily comfortable in character and lifestyle, leading lives as sepia-tinted as their photographs, like retired schoolmasters whiling away pleasant hours in a sociable village setting and becoming increasingly distant from any genuinely rural roots they might once have had. They remained an influence in the village, of course, but they were not *of* the village. You could not imagine the late-Victorian vicar as a smuggler, or eating and drinking with abandon, or being a bold sportsman – though several individuals were indeed ardent members of the local hunt, some keeping their own packs, and the novelist Joanna Trollope remembers her Gloucestershire grandfather as a 'hunting parson' who delivered the parish magazine on horseback.

In 1860 Rector Plenderleath of Cherhill accepted his Wiltshire living against the solemn advice of his uncle who said on no account should he ever drive across the downs unless both he and his servant carried firearms to ward off the notorious Cherhill Gang of highwaymen. Plenderleath heard that, only a few years before his arrival, one of the gang used to carry out his raids in summertime completely naked because, he said, not only did such a sight frighten his victims but also a naked man was less easily recognized.

The 20th century saw a further weakening of the old bonds as the church became less dominant in the village and was gradually eased out of its important welfare role by the State. The Rev. G. Irvine, vicar of Portfield, was feeling the economic pinch in 1916 when he wrote in his parish magazine: 'I thank you once again for your kind Easter offering of £4 10s which was larger by a few shillings than that of last year or any previous year. It may interest you to know that I shall have to pay income tax of about 15s 9d on this amount (being 3s 6d in the £, "earned income"). £4 10s therefore becomes reduced to £3 14s 3d! However, I don't grudge the 15s 9d if it will help finish the war.' Poor vicar: in some parishes he might have expected the Easter offertory plate to collect as much as £200.

The 20th-century vicar lost his way a little, unsure of his relevance in the rural community. Like his forebears at intervals over the centuries, he often found himself trying to serve several parishes at once, rushing from one to the other, his black robes no longer flying in the slipstream of his horse or his bicycle but bundled into the confines of a car which, though it bore him more quickly, further insulated him from his flock – a flock which was itself in a constant state of fluctuation as people became rootless.

There had been something of a fashion among Victorian parsons to make their churches more dignified – more 'Victorian', in fact. Many churches used to have galleries for the village band, be it a group of fiddlers, flautists and trumpeters or, as Thomas Hardy's grandfather had found in 1801, one old man with an oboe. The Victorians, however, decided that bands in church were vulgar and noisy: they dwindled rapidly in mid-century, and the galleries which they had once occupied were pulled down or quietly rotted away as the rumbustious singing of village artisans was replaced by the decorous tinkle of the harmonium, the disciplined swell of the organ and the well-rehearsed harmonies of choirs dressed primly in their white piecrust frills and vestments. Harmoniums were still

A Church Army van spreading the word.

being played in small village churches after World War I and a church at Mulcheney relied on a clockwork instrument until 1907, when it locked itself into permanent play and had to be destroyed.

The band's gallery in the ancient and intriguing little chapel next to the isolated woodland Victorian church on the hangers above my valley was reached by a flight of steps. In the 1860s the incumbent was John Henry Clayton, uncle of the Rev. 'Tubby' Clayton (founder of Toc H), and one Sunday morning there was an ominous creaking from the laden gallery. Clayton's son happened to be visiting home from Australia; he was a burly man and, as his father shouted a warning to the band, he (it is said) held up the sagging gallery with his shoulder while the musicians filed to safety down the steps.

During the 18th century, more than a thousand chapels and meeting houses had been built and some 2400 licences granted to nonconformist movements. Chapel groups appealed to many villagers seeking a more vigorous spirituality and there developed something of a divide between churchgoers and chapelgoers which, varying from amicable to quite hostile, continued and continues even today. In 1885, for example, the Rev. Lefroy Rogers, vicar of Grimston in Yorkshire, refused to allow a grave to be opened for the burial of the child of a Wesleyan. The village was furious: he was assaulted with tin cans and shouting, and his effigy was burned on the village green. However, the parish clerk, who was more in touch with the villagers, ignored his vicar and dug the grave anyway.

Methodism was still strong in Yorkshire in the early years of the 20th century. Harry Etherington, recalling his boyhood spent among the Primitive Methodists around Holderness, remembers that the village boys were more interested in the preachers' clothes than in their highly emotive deliveries, for their excited gesticulations often led to sartorial accidents. A stiffly starched white shirt might be a false front which could slip to reveal an old striped garment underneath, or joy of joys, the standard false cuffs might fly off and land among the congregation. These preachers were familiar local worthies, generally poorly educated and speaking in broad dialect, and on intimate terms with God. Etherington remembers a rugged pig-jobber recommending the power of prayer from his own experience after the loss of his wife. 'Noo Lord,' he had said, on bended knee, 'You mun find me another wife. Fust 'un was nobbut a semmit 'un.'

Frank Bullock would have understood that 'semmit' meant fragile. A Wiltshire gardener married to a lady's maid he had met while in service at a big house, Bullock was described by his son Alan (the noted historian) as a liberal in both politics and religion. He had a talent for oratory and a splendid bass-baritone voice, and the combination soon led him to become a Nonconformist lay-preacher. He had left school at 13 but, when invited to train as a Congregational minister, he ploughed through a monumental amount of studying, working as the squire's orchard gardener by day and reading by oil-lamp until well past midnight. He discovered the works of Thomas Hardy, Ruskin, Browning and Goethe, and passed his exam to qualify for the ministry in 1914. The family was promptly uprooted from rural Wiltshire and transplanted to industrial Lancashire's mining and mill town of Leigh, which must have been a considerable cultural shock for all of them, and thence to Bradford.

Most chapels, though unpretentious, were built of red brick, regardless of the village's local materials and styles, and though they sat a little unhappily in the landscape, they increasingly became social centres in the villages. Chapel was friendly, exciting and active, the sermons were entertaining, the singing lusty and there were fêtes, camp meetings, tea meetings, 'love feasts', temperance festivals, anniversaries – many a chance to play games, share food, show off new clothes and meet old friends. By the late 19th century there were Methodist Guild nights, combining devotions with education, and young men's institutes and mutual improvement societies providing courses in mathematics, English, gymnastics or shorthand. Chapel did not segregate the secular from the religious and it offered what had once been offered by the old festivals and fairs: a calendar of celebrations – though less rough of old, and of course 'dry', but still vigorous.

Some villagers found their own way of dealing with religious problems without the help of chapel or church. An old farm labourer wrote a letter to the devil, firmly but politely telling him that he wanted nothing more to do with him. Did he post his letter? 'A' dug a hole i' the ground, and popped 'un in there,' he confided to a vicar. 'He got it right enough, for he's left me alone from that day to this.'

CHAPTER 4

❧

The Village School

Apart from his religious duties and his relief of the poor, another of the parson's vital roles in many villages was education. Some parsons became the driving force behind the establishment of village schools; some actively taught not only religious instruction but other subjects as well (with varying degrees of success) and very often it was the local vicar who became the village school's inspector, checking that its teaching, equipment and standards were adequate. In pluralist parishes, it was often parish clerks who kept the schools.

The church has always played a leading role in education, in the interests of spreading its own message, and the earliest church schools were established almost as soon as Christianity was brought to these islands. The history of the village school, however, is not a long one and many were built during the Victorian era. In 1818 only one in four children throughout England was receiving any kind of education at all and half the adult population could not read or write their own names. The old grammar schools and public schools were places for the sons of the lord of the manor, the squire and perhaps the more prosperous farmer, but not for the majority of village children. At village level the church was dominant.

In early Victorian times, the choice for village children was between charity schools, dame schools, Sunday schools and schools of industry – all of them voluntarily attended. But for most children, there was no school at all. In countless villages where there was no schoolhouse, the minority of children who did receive education were taught in cottages, vicarages, church naves, barns, farmhouses, almshouses, chapels – or even at the local inn or inside the parish lock-up. Most village parents considered book-learning to be a thorough waste of time, and believed that children learned more by working in the fields or at a cottage industry and contributing to the family's meagre income.

This attitude was deflated a little when religious groups hit upon the idea of holding classes on the only non-working day of the week – Sunday. The Sunday school idea was gladly adopted by Nonconformists as a means of releasing education from the clutches of the established Church and, although Sunday schools left children available to work on weekdays, many squires and gentleman farmers viewed them as centres of sedition and suspected that the education they received there would give the workforce ideas above its station.

OPPOSITE **A group of Wiltshire school children in 1896.**

93

Charity schools, supported by various denominations, supplied the main elementary education. The children were taught the Testaments and good morals, and their primers, writing books and hornbooks were supplied by the charity, which might also give clothes and free bread to the most needy children. Income to support the charity schools came from interest on endowments, voluntary donations and in many cases the 'school pence' each child contributed weekly towards the teacher's salary. Many private individuals provided building plots for schools and many a testator endowed land, the rent from which was to maintain a schoolmaster to teach a specified number of children. The majority of the endowments seem to have been made by clergymen, lords of the manor, squires and clothiers.

In addition to the charity schools there were privately-run dame schools, which initially were set up by quite respectable women who charged a few pence for giving very basic lessons. But some dames had little or no education themselves and were certainly not competent to teach. Many other individuals gave lessons for a few pence in their own homes, be they widows or craftsmen or labourers who had managed to pick up the basics of reading. Yeoman farmer John Ellman of Glynde in Sussex taught his shepherd to read and the man became a voracious reader, taking books with him as he watched over his downland sheep and deriving great pleasure in passing on his skills to other villagers and their children. When he retired from shepherding he became the much-loved village schoolmaster.

Schools of industry were, in theory, intended to prepare children for real life by teaching them the practical and labouring skills which would eventually help them make a living. Some of the earliest were the notorious lace schools, usually held in a crowded cottage room where children as young as three were taught lace-making by a dame. The driving force, however, was not so much for the sake of the children's futures as for the profits of the master merchants who used the 'pupils' as a free labour force. There was a smattering of lessons during the occasional work-breaks when a little reading and writing might be taught, but primarily the school was a sweat-shop, sometimes set up by the parish's Overseers of the Poor. The industries taught in other schools differed according to local customs: in wool-trade country the children learned spinning, weaving and knitting, and in many places girls trained for domestic service.

Of course, in rural areas agriculture was the main field of employment and the work was taught by long experience rather than in any school. The sons of wealthier farmers might be educated at a grammar school but the majority of farmers, like other villagers, had little respect for 'impractical' book-learning, especially if they had to pay for it. But with the rapid improvements in agriculture during the mid 19th century, there was a great increase in the publication of farming books and journals so that education of farmers' sons became more important. New schools were established to offer middle-class boys a general education in preparation for a trade or industry, including agriculture – Framlingham College in Suffolk, for example, was founded in 1863 for the sons of farmers.

For most of the 19th century, education remained voluntary: no child was forced to go to school except by its own parents, and the choice of schools was fairly chaotic. Each community remained free to choose whether or not it would have a school of any kind and how such a school

A lace school in Bedfordshire. Children paid the dame tuppence a week for their training. At home, they worked with their mothers, often by candlelight for maximum productivity.

should be managed and financed. As ever, active local help was the driving force behind the actual building of many a school: villagers supplied voluntary labour and donated the building materials and the site, or contributed money and materials for the day-to-day running of the school – some gave books, or food, or clothing, or perhaps a piano, and others became 'visitors' to teach a lesson or two each week. A body of legislation developed to support two major voluntary societies, both with very long and worthy titles which the general public reduced to single words – the 'British' and the 'National'. The National Society for the Education of the Poor in the Principles of the Established Church was an Anglican movement, while the Nonconformists formed what became the British System for the Education of the Labouring and Manufactory Classes of Society of Every Religious Persuasion, and

Hollycombe School at Wardley, Sussex. Built as a model school on Sir John Hawkshaw's estate in 1869, it was enlarged in 1880 to accommodate up to 142 children.

both societies had considerable influence on village schools.

Not until 1876 did compulsory attendance at what were still voluntary schools become the law of the land and only in 1891 was free education made available to all children up to the age of 14. Local authorities, which took control of primary, secondary and higher schools in 1902, were soon providing free meals to needy children, undertaking medical inspections, encouraging physical training and restricting the employment of school children.

In some villages the introduction of compulsory education was met with indignation. To the villager, long used to self-sufficiency and able to manipulate the apparently dominant lord and squire, whose faces and names were so familiar, government and county councils proved too remote and faceless to be sensitive to his needs. The 1902 Education Act enabled the State to step in and take control

of local education, removing some of the village's independent management of its own affairs. Everything became regulated rather than responsive to village demands and events. School holidays had set dates instead of being arbitrarily declared by the landowners or the vicar and no longer took account of the demands of the land – the harvest and haymaking need for extra labour, for example, were irrelevant to the standardized timetables devised on a national basis. The use of local dialect in school was frowned upon and the country began to lose its rich vocabulary of local words and expressions as children were gradually squeezed into a national mould of speech and thought.

In spite of an Act in the 1870s which attempted to regulate the employment of children in agriculture, many rural schools blithely ignored the various attendance regulations which indeed proved virtually unenforceable. George Dew noted that the chairman of his Board of Guardians, a JP, said he would evade the Act in every way he possibly could, and several of his members agreed with him, which Dew put down to their ignorance and their Toryism (the Act had emanated from a Liberal government). Dew cites many instances of children working: a little boy aged seven, for example, whose mother had been deserted by her husband (several of the Guardians said it benefited children to begin work so young and would do him more good than going to school); the Brock family, of which Dew wrote, when 11-year-old Richard Brock threw a stone at his horse, 'none of this family ever go to school and they are complete pests to the village'; the family of William Golder (whose children were 'too dirty' to be admitted to the schoolroom); and young Edward Tuffrey, aged ten, employed on his father's farm in spite of constant warnings.

Children were no longer supposed to take the tra-

harvest, sheep-shearing, poultry-plucking or beating for the shoot. Real life had to take precedence over mere bookwork! And who could resist the lure of a local fair or a chapel treat? The schools did their best, offering attendance inducements like medallions or pennies (on the Scilly Isles, children paid one penny a week to attend school but tuppence if they didn't!), books and bibles, free clothes and silver watches.

The 'school pence' persisted until schooling became free in 1891. The amount varied – perhaps tuppence or threepence, or as much as ninepence a week – and was each child's contribution towards the school's financial independence. But even tuppence was often beyond larger poor families, though the school committee could waive the pence if it saw fit or could vary the amount according to circumstance. Typically, in 1874 Dr Holme's Charity School at Headley in Hampshire drew up a new scale of fees on a sliding scale: a labourer's child was charged tuppence, a journeyman's threepence, a tradesman's fourpence and a farmer's ninepence, while 12 poor children paid nothing at all. Those were the days when the village still controlled its own affairs and responded to local circumstances and needs.

What, then, was it like to be a child in a Victorian village school? It was not comfortable, for sure. Often the building was extremely cold in winter in spite of the smoking potbellied stove where damp clothes steamed over the lunchtime pasties. The seats were hard, loose wooden planks on iron supports with no back to lean against unless they were fixed to the cold, damp wall. Sanitation was rudimentary at best – a cold-water tap outside and pail-closets across the

ditional day off to join the village's Band of Hope march, or watch a circus caravan passing through, or join the fun of a local farm sale. Yet school log-books show that old habits died hard and there are countless entries showing that half the pupils had failed to attend if there was a call for potato-pickers or crop-weeders, or if help was needed with the yard which stank horribly when they were periodically emptied.

And the sounds. The school bell summoning and releasing you, the scrape of pencils on slates, the scratch of metal nibs, dipped into soot-and-spit ink in brass-capped inkwells set into ink-stained desks where many had carved their initials. Boxes of silvery sand in which the very young first learned to trace out their letters and pot-hooks.

Several of the old charity schools threw in a free uniform as part of their benefactor's endowment, especially if that benefactor was a clothier. In most village schools, however, children simply wore everyday clothes – hand-me-down corduroys or their older sisters' cast-offs for the boys, dresses with pinafores and black woollen stockings for the girls, and uncomfortably sturdy boots for both at school, even if they went barefoot at home.

In terms of lessons, apart from the vicar's daily scripture class, there would, of course, be the 'three Rs', with a heavy emphasis on learning by rote and class-chanting. Multiplication tables to 12 times, the Ten Commandments, the Sermon on the Mount, spelling, copybook writing, needlework; later perhaps a little history, geography and basic science, and in a rural village possibly nature, the weather, agriculture, with practical gardening and poultry-keeping in the schoolyard. By the early 20th century domestic science (cooking, butter-making and laundry) and handicrafts like knitting, stitching and woodwork were added to the curriculum.

Recalling the village school in the 1890s, Miss Anne Coleman of Alton, Hampshire, remembered her first-day task of shredding unbleached calico into heaps of threads, which were then stored in a bag for a later class. For her first sewing lesson, she was handed a six-inch piece of unbleached calico with a tacked hem, its upper part with blue dots and its lower part with red ones. Having learned to thread the needle, she put it into the red dot and brought it out through the blue one – a perfect hem stitch. She then graduated to hemming a blue duster and a red-checked linen tea-cloth. Next came oversewing. The teacher cut out shapes of cats and dogs printed on fine calico and put them in pairs for the girls to sew into animals which they stuffed with the carefully shredded calico threads. Meanwhile, the boys would be reading, learning poetry, history and geography, sharing their books with each other and frequently getting themselves into trouble.

Ruth Mott remembers going to a little red-brick village school across the street just after World War I. There were three classes, all in the same room, and her first day there was spent learning about 'ivy-leafs', as she proudly reported to her father – 'ivy-leaf in God the Father, God the Son and God the . . . .'

The punishments? Take a look at your village school's punishment book and see some of the familiar names of now respected villagers! Les Vale, one of a family of ten, remembers that his own family formed a high proportion of the average attendance of about 68 children at his village school and most of the rest of them were relatives by marriage. There seemed to be a continual race between the mothers: if Mrs Vale had another baby, so did Mrs Clue or Mrs Booker or Mrs Luff – an endless production line which kept the school's three rooms full. Mrs Knight had 11 children, another related family had nine. The school's one master and two teachers certainly had their hands full, as the old punishment books show.

The 'crimes' of 50 to 100 years ago were much as they are today: cheekiness, giggling, making faces, disruption, disobedience, pilfering, breaking the rules and smoking (pipes, not cigarettes then). Punishment was usually by caning with a birch rod kept in water to maintain its whippiness. Less severe was detention (usually in the schoolroom but sometimes in the parish lock-up) or humiliation in the form of having to wear a dunce's cap or a placard hung around the neck.

Some 'teachers' were as young as ten or 11 years old. These were National monitors who helped to teach the little ones, kept children in order and carried out a range of classroom duties like mixing the ink powder, preparing the pens and copybooks, and handing out primers and slates. Mid-19th century teachers were often barely educated themselves; sometimes completely illiterate villagers sought to earn a very few pence by part-time 'teaching' in order to eke out a very low income from other work. Others were those who had failed at another trade. These wholly unqualified teachers varied from the totally incompetent and uncaring to the most dedicated. Often the village teacher was the parish clerk or churchwarden, or a small yeoman, an aged farm labourer or a retired weaver. The pay was terrible, depending on the terms of the endowment and the generosity of the village, and schoolmistresses were paid even less than schoolmasters.

Sometimes, though, the teacher was an outsider with at least a basic education and could bring a wider perspective into the schoolroom and into the village itself. Mary Banfield (1845–1936), born at Westmeston in Sussex, spent two years at the Brighton Training College before she became headmistress of Lower Heyford's village school in 1867. She married in 1872, having first obtained permission from the rector to retain her school on marriage. She proved to be a highly successful teacher. In 1877, for example, over 99 per cent of her pupils 'passed in everything' when the inspector examined them in reading, writing, arithmetic, grammar and geography. When she finally retired in 1913, she laid on a 'good meat tea' for her pupils' mothers, some of whom arrived from neighbouring hamlets in farm wagons.

The Misses Mary and Elizabeth Creek Hore, daughters of a tallow chandler and grocer, kept a ladies' boarding school where George Dew was taught as a boy. He said that 'both of them possessed unswerving firmness of character, amounting almost in some instances to stupidity .... Both are practical Christians, in very word and deed, and neither belong to the Established Church.' They always attended the Methodist Chapel and Miss Mary had become a Baptist as a young woman 'but her view of religion must have been very gloomy for in external behaviour she had all the appearance, save of dress, of a nun; and her friends frequently stated that if she belonged to the Roman Catholic Church no doubt she would have

An infants' class in a council school at Lavenham, Suffolk, in 1915.

Three children enjoying a spot of blackberrying.

doing its best to persuade the squire to pay the new salary personally.

In 1906 a countrywide school meals service was introduced because the general state of children's nutrition was so appalling. At first, health care in schools was non-existent; epidemics were common and it was left to the head teacher to decide whether a child was infectious. Then in 1875 medical officers of health were appointed and district nurses were given the job of checking schools for infectious diseases and inspecting the children's heads for nits and lice.

One little girl would always remember catching scarlet fever in 1901 and being ordered by the doctor into the dreaded fever hospital. She had to wear the clothes she had been wearing the previous day (they would all be burned) and was taken to the hospital, although only five minutes' walk away, in the 'fever cart', an enclosed black van drawn by a very old horse. The hospital in this case was a converted hop kiln, with three large wards (one for boys, one for girls, and a playroom) and an elderly woman as nurse, cook and housekeeper. The children were allowed to play outside in a gravelled yard behind an iron fence and locked gate from where they could watch people walking by and could wave at their family across the road. Six weeks spent in such isolation was a long time for a child, after which time they would be sent home with a 'whole new skin', all the old unwanted skin shed with the help of soda baths.

Many school memories are more pleasant. Old schoolyard games, for example – hopscotch, skipping games, singing and rhyming games, clapping games, knucklebones (or jacks), catching games, tag and so on.

become a most austere nun.' Dew put this unfortunate gloominess down to a disease of the liver and heart (she died at the age of 49) and said that, while not faultless, she was a good woman. Miss Elizabeth, 'a very plain person in appearance', was very deaf.

Many village teachers were eccentric and colourful, just like many village squires and parsons, and they tended to stay in the same job for decades until they were long, long past usefulness and quite devoid of inspiration. But standards were raised as the State became more involved, and HM Inspectors might point out their deficiencies, or suggest the need for an assistant teacher – with the village

Boys, as always, carried stones in their pockets to be thrown at anything and everything. More precious were marbles, when they could be afforded, and there were many marbles games. And there was conquering conkers – cracking your opponent's string-suspended horse chestnut with your own (toughened to a secret recipe); pitch-and-toss with anything from horseshoes to tiddlywinks and buttons; spinning tops and bowling hoops. Other games included makeshift hockey games like Bandy, using a knobbed or crook-ended stick cut from the hedgerow to clout a chunk of wood, or each other, or the slightly more sophisticated Shinty using walking-sticks and a wooden ball. Less sophisticated was pud-fighting which involved flicking gobs of mud at other children with whippy hedgerow canes.

Unlike their urban cousins, village children had the extra freedom of a rural playground – endless woods and meadows through which they wandered on their way to school, catapult and ferret in pocket perhaps, collecting feathers, sucking nectar from clover and honeysuckle flowers, tasting berries and nuts and roots, searching for birds' nests and daring to eat moorhens' eggs, dipping for tadpoles and tickling for minnows in the brook. There was always *plenty* to do in the countryside.

World War I, though fought across the seas, made a considerable emotional impact in the village. Everybody had a son or a brother or uncle or father or cousin in the trenches and some of the 'old boys' came back to tell the village school about their exploits, though many more never came back except as names on the war memorial on the village green. Country children picked tons of black-berries, crab apples, rosehips and horse chestnuts at the government's behest (the conkers were an alternative and highly experimental livestock feed, to release grain for human consumption). They raised money for Our Dumb Friends League to help wounded war horses in France; they knitted socks for sailors and collected eggs for soldiers; they raised money to buy tents for the troops and found time to work in the fields in the absence of so many of the village's menfolk. And they wept for the victims.

A soldier on Christmas leave in 1917.

CHAPTER 5

Village Worthies

The Country Doctor

Witches and 'wise ones' still flourished in mid-Victorian times. Pauper's wife Ann Tustin, who died in 1875 at the age of 79, was generally regarded as a witch, a 'bad, eccentric woman' who boasted of having bewitched her own daughter (the girl died less than a year later). But she did not like the other witches she claimed visited her mud hut in various disguises and, to keep them out, she stuck pins into a sheep's liver and put crossed knives at every crevice through which they might enter. In the same village there was cunning old Jimmy Jagger: if anybody had lost anything, they visited Jimmy to find out who the culprit was. In 1876, a rather delicate 17-year-old girl called Mary Ellen Rouse became a little deranged and her father was convinced she had been bewitched and that he knew who was responsible, though he would not say. Ann Tennant, the sharp-tongued old wife of a shoemaker, was murdered in 1875 by her near neighbour, a farm labourer; she was widely regarded in her village as a witch and whenever livestock died, crops failed or people fell ill, everyone said, 'Hey! old Mother Tennant's at the bottom o' this 'n. 'Tis that evil eye o' hern for sure.'

The 'wise ones' (or 'good witches') were often expert herbalists – and today the most sophisticated of pharmaceutical companies can admit that many of the old remedies were effective. Certainly the country people trusted them and preferred them to most of the new-fangled medicines prescribed by doctors.

At the beginning of the 19th century, professional doctors, city men at heart, began to turn their eyes towards the villages and the growing problem of epidemic diseases like typhoid and cholera which, they suspected, were spread by the increasing tide of stagnant sewage and contaminated drinking-water. In many rural areas during much of the 19th century, privies simply trickled their effluent into open channels between the cottages. Then, in 1849, the earth closet was invented by a vicar in Dorset after a local cholera epidemic, when he discovered that raw sewage had been seeping into the village wells. In 1875 an inspector of nuisances visited a shepherd's cottage where eight people were ill and two already dead from typhoid and took a sample of drinking-water from the cottage's pump. 'The water appeared as if very slightly tinged with soap-suds,' he reported, 'and on holding it up in the bottle before the sun there could be seen an immense quantity of filaments resembling what is sometimes called flue; but the chief feature belonging to the water was a greasy film which immediately settled upon its surface.' Elsewhere he had reason to complain of a privy 'so full that it was overflowing the top of the seat and causing thereby a great nuisance'.

Disease remained a fact of everyday life throughout the 19th century, at all social levels. Children became the victims of regular epidemics of scarlet fever, diphtheria, measles and whooping-cough. Smallpox frequently swept through families and was a persistent killer until it was gradually beaten into submission by a vaccination campaign. The early vaccination methods, however, were almost as dangerous as the disease itself. William Abel Ryder, a grocer, was typical of many who preferred a week in jail rather than let his children's bodies be abused by such 'experiments'.

After the 1850s doctors became increasingly professional but it remained unusual for even a large village to have a resident doctor until the 20th century, by which time he was a respected and hard-working professional, likely to be a good friend of the squire. Young Victorian

BELOW & BELOW LEFT
The village water sources were often a major factor in the disease epidemics of the 19th century. The village stream and parish pump were easily contaminated by seeping sewage.

The 19th-century workhouse was intentionally grim, to encourage the poor to do all in their power to stay out of it – it offered a last resort rather than a stepping-stone to a better life.

doctors found themselves practising in workhouses and asylums for very little money. Typical of them was Thomas Blick, who, having spent a year as house surgeon in a Liverpool workhouse, felt himself quite fortunate when, in 1873 at the age of 32, after nine years as a medical man, he accepted the post of medical officer in a rural district. His salary was £58 per annum, with an extra ten shillings for midwifery cases, out of which he had to pay for his patients' medicines. In 1880 Blick was accused by a patient of being 'beastly drunk', but character witnesses told the magistrates that the doctor had not been seen drunk in the last 12 months and he was let off with a warning. On the whole,

villagers distrusted doctors – especially those armed with surgical knives – and tended to avoid the profession altogether. The poor dreaded illness, as it was a sure and compulsory passport into the dreaded workhouses. As late as the early 1920s, an old man of 73 valiantly fought to keep out of one, telling a magistrate that he only had a scalded leg and that his cottage could not possibly be insanitary as he had lived in it all his life as had his parents, who lived to the ages of 96 and 89, and had reared ten children there with no case of sickness in the family for 60 years.

In truth the 19th-century workhouse was no better than a prison, and even in the 20th century an inmate was more likely to die of broken spirit in the workhouse than of sickness at home. Most local councils, who took over responsibility for the old, the sick and the mentally ill in 1929, found better ways of caring for them, but many of the workhouse buildings were still used as public assistance institutions in the 1940s. There are villagers alive today who can remember those dreary, barren places all too well.

For much of the 19th century and even up to World War I, most villagers preferred familiar herbal remedies either obtained from the local 'wise' woman or which they made themselves. Everybody had their home remedies for minor ailments, and faith in their efficacy was probably just as effective as the powers of the *materia medica*. If these failed, they would resort to the market-town apothecaries, who liked to travel through country districts during the summer but stayed snugly behind their shop counters in winter, sending out remedies by post.

Quack doctors abounded. They claimed to cure every conceivable complaint in man or beast, and many a village had its resident quack, who bottled his own secret mixtures with a dash of herbs and often a dash of the scriptures for good measure. An old man, after reeling off a list of his herbal remedies (including rubbing 'wapse' stings with nettles), related the tale of a renowned doctor who left a sealed book, not to be opened until after his death, whereupon it was to be auctioned. After paying £600 for it the proud owner opened this treasure-trove of medicine with trembling hands. Within was but a single piece of advice: 'Always remember to keep the feet warm and the head cool.' By the 1920s quacks and the equally familiar itinerant tooth-pullers had disappeared.

Childbearing was a constant condition in the life of most village women and they would have been shocked at the idea of birth control. Agricultural workers and their wives were, it seems, particularly fertile. One example, and there are many, is that of Sarah Powell of Bucknell, Oxfordshire, who gave birth to 23 children, including six sets of twins and one of triplets. At one stage Sarah produced five children in 11 months. Seven were still alive when she was 51 but by then her husband, a farm labourer, was 'lame and ruptured and quite unable to work'.

Even if the opportunity had been offered her, the Victorian village woman would not have considered going into a hospital to give birth. Birth was not an illness; it was an annual event that took place at home, with the help of relatives and neighbours, or a local woman who had made midwifery her calling and whose experience was considerably greater than her training and qualifications. Before legislation in 1902 introduced national standards of midwifery, many midwives had been thoroughly disreputable – unskilled, untrained, negligent, given to malpractice and with no understanding of hygiene. But the midwife had always been a familiar figure, often owing not a little of her knowledge and status to the traditional village 'wise woman'. In any case, most villagers worried even less about hygiene than she did.

Even in the 1930s most births still took place at home

'Rough Jimmy' Minns, born at Ditchingham, Norfolk, in 1826 and photographed in 1901 splitting spars for thatching. He had become infirm in his old age but was so distressed at the prospect of the workhouse that the local squire gave him a cottage and a shilling a week for the rest of his life.

and most women relied on the services of 'the nurse'. People paid perhaps tuppence a week to belong to their local nursing association so that they could call out the district nurse when they needed her. As few people had a telephone, very often the husband or friend of a woman in labour would jump on a bike and pedal furiously to the nurse's home in the hope that she was there.

Nurse Wake of South Harting, a Sussex village just below the South Downs, in the 1930s.

By the end of the 1920s, however, local councils had become generally more involved in community health care, seeking to educate mothers, tackling the scourge of tuberculosis, setting up school health clinics and gradually improving local water supplies and sewage disposal. Even so, in 1938 more than a quarter of England's rural parishes had no piped water and nearly half had no mains sewage system. Most families still used earth closets or garden privies, although many council houses had tap water and some even had indoor water closets connected to small sewage plants nearby.

Even in the early 1950s a significant proportion of rural

homes had no piped water, no WC and no fixed bath. In the Yorkshire village of Flamborough, the whole community's water was supplied by an iron hand-pump: the water was pumped into a large water-cart and sold to the villagers at a penny a bucketful. In a certain Wiltshire village, the *Sunday Graphic* noted in the year that parish councils were formed that there was only one well for the whole community. It belonged to the public house, which charged villagers a ha'penny a bucket. The same article pointed out that many villages still relied on 'a stream of more than doubtful purity' for their water supply, but that in others enterprising individual landowners had erected standpipes at convenient distances, or even piped good water to individual cottages. In Dinton, Wiltshire, the local lord of the manor constructed a private reservoir in 1904 to provide his tenants with piped water although the rest of the village continued to use wells, pumps or ponds until mains water arrived in 1958.

The Village Bobby

The friendly village bobby only a short history, dating from the second half of the 19th century, though he had a predecessor of sorts in the old parish constable, a title which had been used since medieval times for one of four principal parish officers who were elected annually – the other worthies being the churchwarden, the surveyor of highways and the overseer of the poor. The constable's status diminished rapidly when wealthier villagers became reluctant to accept the post and eventually only the unemployed (or unemployable) took the job, most of them illiterates unable to read a warrant and this was typical of parish constables for most of the 19th century. Unloved and disrespected, they had become men in menial posts nobody else wanted.

One of the old constable's duties had been to look after

The parish lock-up, just big enough for one offender.

the village stocks. The essence of this punishment was public humiliation: you were shackled in full view of everybody in the village, all of whom knew you and your entire family. The use of stocks lingered here and there until the mid 19th century, although in 1879 Samuel Venemore of Wendlebury could remember only one case during his lifetime, that of a drunken traveller who had been put in the village stocks and had a bucket of cold water thrown over him to sober him up. In the 1850s, the parish constable at Stokesley decided to refurbish the stocks: some of the locals rioted but others thought it an excellent idea and repaired them. In 1853, Jim Brigham of Beverley, Yorkshire, found drunk on a Sunday by some churchmen, was put in the stocks but, sympathizing with him, the crowd gave him a pipe of tobacco to while away the time. As late as 1872 Mark Tuck, a habitual drunkard from Newby, spent four hours in the stocks and was mocked by a laughing, booing crowd.

The principle of humiliation was at its most effective (and spiteful) in the 'rough music' with which villagers showed their disapproval of lack of sexual morals, especially adultery and wife-beating. In 1867, a woman whose husband was in prison for debt committed adultery with George Coggins, a baker, in the carriage of a stationary train. They were seen by a railway guard who spread the gossip around the villages, and for three consecutive evenings their separate homes were serenaded by a cacophony of banging on metal utensils, with much shouting and jeering – which was little consolation to Mrs Coggins. Finally, effigies of the offenders were carried around their respective villages, mounted on poles – the man dressed in a baker's apron and the woman in crinoline and bonnet – and were then set on fire to the continuing clatter and rattle of the 'rough music'. There are cases of this type of village justice even in the 20th century.

While human miscreants were placed in the stocks or in the tiny parish lock-up, wandering livestock would be placed in the village pound to await collection by their owners. Some pounds were no more than pleach-fenced enclosures, long since vanished, but others were more substantial walled pens which might now be part of a garden with only the name 'Old Pound' recalling its original role. The Yorkshire moorland village of Hutton-le-Hole, where pounds were known as pinfolds, had a small, square, sturdy pound built of stone and supervised by a pinder, who collected the relevant fines and pound fees when animals had been allowed to stray. In 1879 old Thomas Worvill, the parish poundsman or hayward of Islip, took charge of three straying colts but his pound had long since been demolished and he had to enclose them next to the pub. He had been sworn in as poundsman nearly a quarter of a century earlier when, among other duties, he ensured that no wheelbarrows were left about the village at night – because once upon a time 'Lady' Buckland, the rector's snooty wife, had fallen over a stray barrow in the dark.

In the 1830s, when for a century the only effective rural policing had been by voluntary protection societies formed by groups of tradesmen to fend off highwaymen and migrant criminals, a royal commission found that the rural constabulary was totally incompetent, its men not only illiterate but also thoroughly dissolute and frequently blind-drunk, causing nothing but mockery from criminals. The County and Borough Police Act of 1856 eventually compelled the counties to establish rural forces and empowered them to take over parish lock-ups and station houses. Yet old-fashioned part-time parish constables persisted in some places until as late as 1881.

The new rural policeman of the 1870s was a better man than the old dissolute constable. The job was respectable and secure, and attracted unskilled labourers who would otherwise have worked in the fields, factories or mines. They were required to be intelligent, able to read and write, active, of a strong constitution and certified free of 'bodily complaints', at least 5 ft 7 in. tall and not more than 40 years old. They also had to be recommended as of irreproachably good moral character and connections. Overall, the village bobby's lot was not a happy one. Discipline was very strict, the work was hard, and wages were as low as those of an unskilled agricultural labourer. They had to attend church on Sunday, and while some chiefs insisted on chastity, others merely limited the number of children in a constable's family to two. They were also discouraged from eating and drinking with 'civilians' and from entering pubs or beerhouses except in the course of their duties, and could certainly not get themselves drunk – which ruled out most of the old parish constables, though one of the latter in Devon took considerable satisfaction in arresting a new-style police-man for drunkenness.

The early uniform consisted of a dark blue swallow-tail coat, a glazed stovepipe top hat, white duck trousers for summer and blue serge for winter, an oilskin cape, a staff or baton, a pair of handcuffs, a rattle, a button-brush, an instruction book, and a cutlass for night patrols. A smart appearance was deemed to be most important and many men were ordered to wear whiskers to complete the image.

A Victorian country policeman worked a seven-day week and a ten or 12-hour-day in two shifts. By the 1870s he was lucky to get one rest-day in every four to six weeks, and an annual week's holiday – unpaid. He spent most of his day foot-patrolling for miles on rough rural lanes, on the principle of preventing crime by being a uniformed presence, alert for common offences like 'riding without reins', sheep-stealing, petty larceny, drunkenness, poach-ing and vagrancy; he would check for disorderly behaviour in pubs or at cockfights and prize fights; he kept a sharp eye on the multitude of tramps, thugs, beggars, conmen, thieves and pedlars that passed through his parish; and he did his best to keep gangs from rival villages apart.

As the era rolled on the rural policeman was given

A village policeman, *c.* 1910.

extra duties and he became an inspector of everything conceivable. To make sure he was never idle, he also ran the local fire brigade and ambulance, whitewashed the lock-up, switched on the street lamps and took on the old watchman's role of calling up early risers. To prove that he was diligent in his foot-slogging, he often had to leave tickets at respectable houses in evidence that he had passed by on his beat. With the arrival of the motor car his duties grew. As early as 1901 there was mutual distrust between policemen and motorists, not helped by the fact that most chief constables preferred horses. Speeds were checked with a stopwatch and in 1905 the newly-formed Automobile Association began to warn motorists of speed-traps.

Some police constables were too zealous for the liking of villagers. In 1929 the bobby in the Surrey village of Chiddingfold, well known for its November bonfire night for a century and a half, arrested a group of schoolboys for letting off home-made fireworks in the road. The magistrate fined them £2 each. The village was shocked at the harshness of the arrest and the fines, and, anticipating more trouble from the local lads, extra police were drafted in. That same evening the crowd burned an effigy of a policeman on the bonfire and the Riot Act was read. A few days later the indignant villagers threw their police sergeant into the village pond, after which he did not stay long in Chiddingfold. The village had shown who was really in charge.

Guy Fawkes night has often been the occasion for serious fires, some accidental, others not. In the 1870s the paper mill at Hampton Gay was destroyed by fire one 5 November and rumour had it that the proprietor was quite happy to let it burn while the village was distracted by its own celebrations. Rick fires were common, too, sometimes the result of spontaneous combustion when damp hay overheated, but often enough by deliberate arson. George Dew recalled great excitement in neighbouring villages when a fire burned for two or three hours, lighting up the sky for miles around: it proved to be a straw rick belonging to one Richard Coggins, a farmer and timber dealer, and was probably started deliberately by a disgruntled labourer. The Bicester and Steeple Aston fire-engines were summoned and arrived shortly after the fire broke out but found that there was no water supply within half a mile. They could do nothing but let the rick burn to the ground. The case was unusual in that, more commonly, the brigade took so long to arrive that the rick or building was destroyed before they did so.

In the event of fire there was generally good co-

A couple devastated after a farm fire in the 1920s. The village policeman was often responsible for the co-ordination of fire-fighting.

operation between neighbouring parishes (only a few of which provided fire-fighting equipment for local use) and the private brigades set up by larger estates. Most villages, however, had to rely on voluntary town brigades, which used fire-engines drawn by horses hired from local tradesmen when required. The volunteers often found it quicker to manhandle the engine to the scene of the fire rather than wait for available horsepower. In 1901, the parish council of Castor, Northamptonshire, decided to purchase its own fire-engine and appointed William Carter of Ailsworth as captain of its new brigade. Its first call came in July 1903, when two thatched cottages at Upton were struck by ball-lightning. The brigade was still very active in the 1920s and lightning was again the problem when two of Mr Fitzwilliam's cottages at Marholm were totally destroyed. In 1927, Castor resolved to purchase a motor fire-engine. By about 1910 most of the town brigades had turned from horses to steam power and after World War I several began to use motor vehicles to tow their steam engines before finally converting to petrol power.

A man-powered fire-engine, c. 1910.

The Village Pub

Most English villages have a 'pub', but within living memory even small villages often had several drinking places, be they inns or ale-houses. The numbers of publicans, inn-keepers and beer-sellers were very high in the early Victorian years, though most were part-timers with a second trade.

The genuine inn was much more than a drinking place: it offered food, a bed for the night and accommodation for its guests' horses, and it became something of a community centre for doing business, fixing contracts and deals, making payments, finding jobs, haggling with traders and so on. Most inns flourished on the road to somewhere more important.

The real 'local' was the village ale-house, which had been common even in Anglo-Saxon times; indeed, so much so that in the 10th century King Edgar limited villages to one ale-house each. In 1801, Arthur Young declared: 'Go to an ale-house kitchen of an old-enclosed country, and there you will see the origin of poverty and high poor-rates. For whom are they to be sober? For whom are they to save? For the Parish? If I am diligent, shall I have leave to build a cottage? If I am sober, shall I have land for a cow? If I am frugal, shall I have half an acre of potatoes? You offer no motives; you have nothing but a parish officer and a workhouse! – Bring me another pot.'

Ale-houses were ordinary farmhouses and cottages

ABOVE **The King's Arms, a Dorset village inn.**

RIGHT **'Rustics' eyeing a new phonograph with suspicion in the 1920s.**

OPPOSITE **The village pub in Graffham, Sussex, in the 1920s.**

doing the cider rounds in his youth before World War I, when almost every local cottage in the widely scattered hamlets around his village brewed its own cider and offered it for general tasting. Even today, when these isolated cottages are no more than a memory of broken bricks occasionally turned up by the plough, their twig-tangled old apple trees sometimes hide in the hedgerows and surprise you in the early autumn with an abundance of small, colourful, inedible apples of many forgotten old varieties.

In the 1870s, licensed houses remained thick on the ground: in Sussex, for example, they averaged one for every 176 people in the county and most villages had at least two or three pubs. But many rural pubs were struggling in the wake of mass migrations of villagers into the towns and it was with relief that the country pub opened its emptying arms to welcome tourists who began to come out of the towns in search of fresh air on their bicycles and later their motorcycles and cars.

whose inhabitants sold their home-brew in the kitchen or living-room to local people, who came to relax and chat as they drank. Some of the more successful ale-houses gradually expanded their premises to accommodate more and more villagers, many of whom paid for their drinks in kind rather than in cash. Houses near communal meeting-places such as the green or the forge fared best and there was a real boom for the ale-houses when the railways were being built and thirsty navvies crowded the countryside. Numerous ale-houses were ripe for picking by the rapidly developing and technologically advanced brewing industry, which soon managed to force most home-brewers into giving up or being taken over.

In apple-growing regions, ale-houses sold rough cider as well. Woodsman Sid Kingshott fondly remembered

By 1914 all but a handful of pubs had become tied to large breweries. Pub or inn – call it what you will – it was a venue where coroners held inquests, where magistrates would meet, taxmen collected dues, political parties held election meetings, local councils had meetings and dinners, and where concerts and other entertainments took place. The 'public house' (a term first used in 1850 precisely because it had become the local meeting-place) had stepped in to fill the gap between the church nave of the past and the village hall of the future as a shelter for communal activities.

The Village Shop

The traditional method of shopping for occasional household goods in rural areas was to acquire them direct from village craftsmen and producers, or to walk to the nearest weekly town market or a fair, or to make use of an assortment of itinerant traders who regularly called round the villages over the weeks and months, or to use the village carrier.

The carrier, with his horsedrawn tilt-cart or covered wagon, was the main link between village and town. He often began the service as an offshoot to a main trade which already involved him in the regular transportation of his own goods to market. He might be a miller or a farmer, perhaps, or a domestic coalman collecting fuel from the nearest railway depot for house-to-house delivery. Many carriers continued to run a second trade and there were countless farmer/carters, many shopkeepers and publicans with part-time carrier businesses and a large number of blacksmiths, who were masters of diversification. Here and there, old trade directories reveal village carriers who were also, for example, 'cowkeeper/coalman' or even 'hairdresser/newsagent'.

Carriers took village goods to market on their pro-

ducers' behalf and brought back goods for those who ordered them from town, be they huge boxes or a packet of pins or a collected debt. And there were 'egglers' or 'higglers' who went round the local farms and cottages collecting eggs, poultry, butter and similar produce to sell in town.

Most villagers had neither the time nor inclination to travel to town themselves as shoppers but carriers often fitted rough benches as seats for those who wanted to make the trip. The number of carriers grew considerably during Victorian times and by the 1880s (when only one in six

OPPOSITE **A 1920s village carrier in Sussex. The carrier played an important role in village life.**

BELOW **Higglers collected poultry and dairy produce to sell in town.**

Itinerants visited the villages selling cheap goods they had bought in bulk from the cities and towns: haberdashery, matches, scent, toys, ironmongery, songsheets, almanacs and what-have-you.

villages had its own railway station) there were at least 200,000 of them. They were still well loved and well used by villagers in the 1920s, when Ruth Mott remembers using the carrier's cart to travel from her Berkshire village into Reading. It was only 12 miles but took three or four hours because of frequent stops to take small personal orders for balls of string, bags of flour and so on.

Itinerants continued to visit the villages regularly to sell their wares and skills and remained an important element of everyday village life throughout the 19th century. They came on foot (pedlars), or on ponies and donkeys (hawkers), or in nag-drawn carts, and the broad term for these wandering men and women was 'chapmen'. They sold all sorts of useful items which the village could not or did not produce for itself, or offered repair services such as tinkering. In 1871, it was estimated that there were about 45,000 pedlars and hawkers in the country and in some places their ratio to the population was as high as one in ten. One part of Gloucestershire, beyond Stroud, became known affectionately as 'Neddyshire' for the number of pack-donkeys distributing goods to the locals.

Arthur Gibbs was familiar with an old-fashioned hawker in the 1890s, a strange-looking half-wit with a slouching gait and a mouldy wideawake hat, who led a donkey and cart and was accompanied by a couple of highly trained lurchers. He was probably a poacher, or at least a poachers' 'fence', though the local keeper kept quiet on that subject. A generation earlier there had also been fish-and-salt sellers whose carts were pulled by teams of dogs, causing uproar and chaos by setting off every barking dog in the neighbourhood as they arrived. They would let their own dogs roam freely about the village, finding whatever food they could while their master had a meal and a drink at the inn or ale-house. When he was ready to leave, the seller would blow a horn and his pack would return to him to be harnessed again. The use of dogs as draught animals was banned in 1854, not because it was considered cruel to the dogs (though they were often treated abominably) but because of complaints about the nuisance and the noise.

Other visitors were more welcome and villagers could buy better quality goods sold by cheapjacks who toured the markets in a very wide rural area around the cities with cartloads of knives, tools, garden spades, pots and pans, leather bridles, horse-whips and so on. George Swinford, living in Filkins, Oxfordshire, remembered how in the 1880s and 1890s a Sheffield cutlers' agent would arrive every spring and autumn, his covered wagon drawn by a pair of big black horses. He would stay in the area for a month, driving from farm to farm during the day and setting up on the village green in the evening so that the villagers could buy billhooks, hoes, pocket knives and other cutlery. On the first evening he spread out his wares near the pub and paid local lads a penny or two to broadcast news of his arrival around the village, gleefully ringing a bell as they did so.

Occasionally an early Victorian village might have a grocer but in the original sense of the word – one who deals in goods by the gross – and frequently such a grocer was also a draper. More specialist was Case the Draper, in Milborne St Andrew, Dorset, whose shop remained for several decades much as it had been in the 1850s and 1860s, with some of the old stock still lying there. Charles Case, son of the original proprietor, was a virtual 'double' of his contemporary, the Salvation Army's 'General' Booth, with his military bearing, broad high forehead, prominent nose, piercing eyes and flowing white beard. Case presided over a generous mahogany counter, cedar-lined drawers, beaver box-hats, shepherd's plaid, gloves, handkerchiefs, threads, needles, pins, ribbons, tapes,

millinery – and a precious stock of the famous covered buttons made in local cottages. This major Dorset cottage industry allowed a wife to make almost as much money as her farmworker husband until it was killed almost overnight in the early 1860s by the invention of machine-made buttons.

There were a few village chemists and druggists, the one offering remedies based on chemicals and the other based on drugs from plants and animals. Chemists included 'tonic wines' among their merchandise and it was therefore natural for them to extend their range by acting as wine merchants, which they often did until well into the 20th century. Ted Mills was an apprentice in a country chemist's before the Great War and remembers selling

Itinerants also offered services such as tinkering and knife-grinding. Here a tinker is mending metal utensils at his camp.

"Old Tins to mend."

laudanum by the ounce to those who wanted it, no questions asked. Opium addicts were not unusual, but laudanum was more innocently the universal cough-mixture for all the family – mixed at home with paregoric, peppermint, aniseed, black treacle and hot water. Mills also sold blue unction (a mercury ointment to keep bed-fleas away), loose jalap and aloes and hiera-picra as purgatives, Epsom salts in great volume for constipated villagers and their cattle, and yellow diachylon for melting with hot water and spreading on cloth as sticking plaster – or making into pills to procure an abortion. In addition, Ted sold cheap perfumes, lavender water, eau de cologne, face powder, parma violets, carmine for rouge, Glauber's salts, bicarb, cream of tartar, linseed oil, turps, spices, vinegar, meths, copper sulphate seed dressing, physic balls for horses, condition powders, udder ointments, drenches for cows, and mange ointments for dogs. Working from eight in the morning until eight at night – 10 pm on Saturdays – Ted had one half day free on Thursdays, if he was lucky.

The spread of the new railway system during the 19th century resulted in the arrival of a wide range of mass-produced items into the heart of the countryside. With quickly-falling prices for once-luxury imported goods like tea and sugar, most villagers could now afford them and wanted to buy them regularly. Village shops began to stock them and other affordable household goods like factory-made biscuits, chocolates, cutlery, cottons and cheap china, and the demand for village shops grew, reaching its peak in about 1880. These shops were really emporiums, selling everything that the village needed under the same roof, rolling into one the bakery, grocery, butcher's shop, ironmonger's, haberdashery, draper's and all.

Miss Heath's farmhouse front-room village shop at Wardley, Sussex, started as a butcher's shop and granary on a farm which raised cattle, pigs and chickens. Soon the shop hit upon the splendid idea of selling their own pigmeal to all the cottagers who kept family pigs, which most of them did. The pig would get bigger and bigger on its meal until the cottager could no longer afford to feed it so the animal was sold to the shop, where it was slaugh-

Cottagers boarding the carrier's cart on their way to market.

tered and then butchered, hung on hooks from the dairy ceiling and cured in big slate salt-containers. Bacon was smoked in a large baconloft above the huge inglenook fireplace. Gradually the shop extended its range: by 1900 it was still selling home-killed pork and bacon but it was also trading as baker, grocer, tea dealer, provision merchant and ale-seller. It stocked china, glass and earthenware, cornmeal and hops, ironmongery and tinware, boots and shoes, and all kinds of furniture – new, second-hand and 'antique'. Miss Heath continued to sell boots and shoes until 1936, though thereafter it became a more straight-forward village grocery.

Miss Heath's was not the only shop in this small village. There was Bennett the cobbler up the hill, Aburrow's post office, bakery and grocery at another farmhouse whence old Mr Taylor and Wally Booker delivered the bread, and a boot-and-shoe shop on the green. This was presided over by old Luckins, who, although stone deaf, still played in the village band, which knew only one tune and lured the villagers with its music once a week to the tap-room so that they could get drunk and settle up their weekly accounts. In addition there was Percy who ran a shop of sorts in his front room (chiefly food); there was a sweet-shop down the lane near the school and a blacksmith's on the green which sold hardware. The population served by all these shops was only a few hundred before the two World Wars, most of them employed on the three large estates that owned everything in the valley including the shop buildings.

Though Wardley still had many of its shops in living memory – and villagers now in their seventies remember them well – today there is not a single shop in the parish for a population of more than a thousand. Many Victorian villages would have sympathized: a sixth of Oxfordshire's rural parishes had no village store in 1891 and the situation was worse in sparsely populated areas. However, old trade directories confirm that many Victorian villages had several shops – butcher, baker, bootmaker, perhaps a tailor, and a general stores where you could buy every-thing from bread to birdseed, horseshoes and linoleum.

Shopkeepers bought in bulk and the goods were usually loose, packed in barrels, chests and sacks with no wasteful individual packaging – customers brought their own containers to fill up with a penn'orth of what they needed. The shopkeeper cut and scooped and weighed and bundled and paper-bagged according to the customer's requests; each shop would grind the coffee beans, blend its own mix of teas to suit the local water, hand-slice the bacon and the soap, cut the tobacco wads and sugarloafs and salt blocks, sieve the dried fruit and rice to remove debris. Most shopkeepers worked very long hours indeed: service to the customer mattered, and most village shops stayed open most weekdays until 7 or 8 pm, and as late as 11 or midnight on Saturdays – as long as there were still villagers spending their wage packets.

The majority of village shops, however, were merely part-time trades conducted from a cottage front room, run by a widow or spinster who was summoned into her domain by the call of 'Shop!' or the jangle of the spring-hung door bell. Farmers, publicans, brewers and carriers might run part-time shops, too, in the typical passion (and economic need) to diversify, and it was people like these, rather than full-time shopkeepers, who seized the opportunity of running a post office in parallel with their main trade when contracts were first offered in the 1840s and 1850s. Gradually more shopkeepers saw the advantages and by the 1850s about half the village post offices were linked with shops. When the village shop boom began to slide in the early 1920s, it was those with a post office section which were best placed to survive.

Diversification remained vital and many village shop-

A butcher's shop (left) and bakehouse in Chapel Street, Robin Hood's Bay, Yorkshire, in the 19th century.

keepers were hard to classify. Just after World War I, Ernest Pulbrook mentions saddlers selling eggs and fruit, butchers selling dairy produce and vegetables, grocers offering seeds and materials. By then shopkeeping was often more a hobby than a business, a useful sideline that kept its proprietor in touch with local gossip.

Even in the 1920s there were still many specialist village shops like butchers and bakers. Retail butchers were common in Victorian villages with as few as 200 inhabitants, selling their own fattened animals on the hoof to wholesale dealers and drovers. In the Surrey village of Chobham, old Ma Tanner the butcher continued to maintain the family's fieldful of pedigree Aberdeen-Angus cattle until she died in the 1970s. Tanner's home-reared prime beef, properly reared and properly hung after slaughter, had been renowned since at least the turn of the century and she also sold superb lamb, bacon, ham and home-made sausages.

Les Vale can remember his local watermill still grinding corn in the 1930s. Part of the millhouse was a bakery where, as a lad, Les baked doughnuts at 4 am at first for sale at the shop and later for delivery by his father, who had set up his own business with horse and cart. This was later replaced by a bicycle and finally by a motor van in the classic upright style of the period, with his name 'and Son' handsomely painted on the side.

In the inter-war period door-to-door deliveries were common – the local farmer's milk rounds with a small boy or elderly man carrying cans of fresh milk, farm butter wrapped in a white cloth and a basket of eggs, and the carts of butchers, grocers, oilmen and ironmongers, fish hawkers, tinkers, chair-menders, and the ice-cream barrow which in winter sold baked potatoes and hot chestnuts.

The thriving village shop felt the first draught of its coming troubles as the 20th century loomed. With increased mobility, villagers could more easily shop in towns where prices were lower, the range of goods was wider and where

FAR LEFT **Milk was not often a feature of the 19th-century villager's diet but was much in demand in the nearby towns. Deliveries were often by old men carrying cans on a yoke.**

LEFT **Advertising signs began to spread into the villages with the increase in literacy.**

they could soon dispose of their growing incomes on goods which the newly literate generation saw advertised in national newspapers and magazines.

Advertising paid. Villagers became consumers rather than producers. No longer content with loose goods in their village shops, they demanded brand names and packaging and a degree of processing in their foods. To compete with the town, village shops began to enliven their windows, fronts, walls and counters with brand-name advertisements on enamelled plaques. By the 1890s the village street face was blanketed with bright colours and bold lettering. Art, of a kind, came to the countryside.

Since the 1880s village shops had also begun to stock newspapers and magazines. In some cases this useful sideline became the shop's main business, supplemented by the sale of sweets and tobacco. Throwing away their clay pipes, villagers began rolling their tobacco into cigarettes instead, though machine-made cigarettes became increasingly popular after World War I.

For children, of course, sweets were more exciting than tobacco. Picture a stone-built sweet-shop, its small-paned windows full of treats to lure children in through the welcoming door with its springy bell triggered by the opening. Inside, great big glass jars of loose sweets of every kind: boiled sweets like jewels, black liquorice sticks, striped humbugs, bulging gob-stoppers changing colour as you sucked through the sugary layers, jellybabies, gumdrops, toffee apples, pastilles, Refreshers, triangular packets of lemon sherbert powder with liquorice-stick dippers, Polo Mints, parma violets, aniseed balls, barley-sugar twists, butterscotch, mintcake, peppermint creams, red-tipped sugar cigarettes, sugar mice with string tails, sugar pigs, treacle toffee, fudge, caramels, pear drops, Turkish delight, bulls-eyes and scented cachous. Before 1939, some shops made their own confectionery and sold it from handcarts at the local market, by the paper bag or twist for a penny a quarter.

Countless pre-war villagers knew little glory-holes like these, and countless more were on name terms with those who served behind the counters of the village grocery and post office. We have now almost lost our village shops and, while their passing might not be mourned in terms of the local economy, they performed a far more important role often overlooked in the emphasis on profitable business. The village shop was a casual meeting-place for the whole village, of all ages and classes. It was a place where the lonely found company and enjoyed the exchange of gossip as they perched on an old wooden chair or upturned barrel thoughtfully provided by the shopkeeper, while customers waited for their goods to be weighed and sorted. Though itinerants had brought news from the wider region and the nation, it was in the shop that the much more important local gossip was spread. And it is gossip, however much it might be despised, that keeps people in touch with each other's misfortunes and binds a community together. The village shop has always been more of a social service than a business.

The Village Garage

When the motor car came into (or through) the village, it needed fuel. Fuel for householders – mostly paraffin for

A typical 1920s petrol filling station, at Fittleworth, Sussex, also offering repairs.

country bus service based in the village. Garages soon became outlets for the huge oil companies, whose blazons began to intrude in the countryside. The familiar scallop shell, for centuries the symbol and utensil of pilgrims, became a glowing yellow sign that indicated the sale of petrol – a national sign, recognized in every part of the country like the other brand names that had invaded villages and had begun the ever increasing trend to standardization.

The Village Workshop

Villages are now such quiet, empty places during the day – even the cars dwindle to a trickle while village commuters are away at their work. Yet before the age of the car, villages were busy, bustling, noisy places for most of the daylight hours. Although many villagers would have been away from the village centre, working in the fields or on the big estate by day, there were many who worked in the heart of the village, supplying the useful items it needed. Workshops formed part of the streetscape and kept the village alive with the physical sounds, smells and activity of their crafts.

In some regions, villages were as much industrial as agricultural. The Staffordshire metal-workers, for example, the clayland potteries and brickyards, villages with quarries or mines or papermills, the village shoemakers of Northamptonshire, the framework knitters of Nottinghamshire and Leicestershire; Yorkshire's wool mills and handloom weavers, wealden iron-working and glass-making villages, lead-mining in Derbyshire, collieries in the Forest of Dean, basket-makers near wetlands where osiers and rushes grew, chairmakers, bell foundries, maltsters, silk mills, skinyards where hides were cured (so smelly that they were banished well away from the cottages), flint-knappers – all over the countryside the

lighting – was sold by various local shops and by roundsmen. In due course some traders – especially hardware shops, saddlers, wheelwrights and blacksmiths – also began stocking petrol for motor vehicles, each laboriously using hand-operated pumps to fill the cans. Many blacksmiths, already involved in the repair of farm machinery, naturally extended their services to motor vehicles and, as the agricultural trade began to dwindle and as electrically operated petrol pumps came into use, quite often the old forge became a filling station. So, eventually, villages saw a completely new enterprise: the garage. Sometimes it was little more than a filling station; sometimes it undertook repairs; sometimes it also ran a tourist teashop, or was part of a more ambitious carrier's business which became a land was alive with people at work within and near their villages.

On a smaller scale, most Victorian villages still depended heavily on their own blacksmiths and farriers, wheelers and carpenters. Larger villages had their own millers, masons, thatchers, shoemakers, tailors and dressmakers to supply their necessities.

❧

Born in 1787, the daughter of a country doctor, Mary Russell Mitford lived as a child in a fine Georgian house in the Hampshire village of Arlesford. By the time she had turned 20 the family occupied a very small labourer's cottage at Three Mile Cross in Berkshire, due to her father's unfortunate passion for gambling away his wife's dowry. In *Our Village*, a collection of her writings first published between 1824 and 1832, Miss Mitford takes her readers on a paper tour of Three Mile Cross, which was to change little over the following 50 years. She describes the home and little shop of the shoemaker, a craftsman well enough off to employ three journeymen (two lame, the third a dwarf), almost opposite the home of the blacksmith, a man with eight children who was 'a high officer in our little state, nothing less than a constable', but whose love of ale meant that the blacksmith-constable was usually the cause of an affray rather than its policeman. Next was the village shop and on the other side the inn, then a collar-maker's shop where horses came to be fitted for their harnesses, then the carpenter's workshop and the wheeler's shop and, beyond, the mason's yard. Along the lane that climbed the hill, beyond a fine farmhouse, was a common scattered with lesser farmhouses and cottages, including the home of the estate's gardener, whose wife was the local

laundress. Other cottagers included a mole-catcher, several duck-rearers and goose-crammers and a splendid quack doctor who had learned his cures from his great-aunt Bridget, the village's long-deceased wise woman.

So there it was, a village full of the bustle and noise and murmur of busyness, people physically working at their crafts in workshops along the street or in outhouses by cottages scattered along the lanes. And so it continued well after Miss Mitford's death in 1855, until the combined Victorian onslaughts of mass production, standardization, faster transport and shrinking village populations caused many of the crafts to fade away.

All over the country, the people who worked in iron and wood were the village's fundamental craftsmen. The

A carpenter/ undertaker's yard near the Scottish borders. As the demand for horsedrawn agricultural vehicles declined, many wheelers became general carpenters, making field gates, wooden household articles and coffins.

Wood formed the basis of many village, cottage and coppice industries and carpentry was an important skill.

blacksmith used to be the king, only a few steps below the squire and the parson and at the top of his class of craftsmen and traders. He made his presence known not just through his necessarily bulky physique but also by the ringing sounds of metal on metal, the rain of sparks, the hot glow and smoke of his fires. The forge was often conve- niently placed near the inn or an ale-house; watching the blacksmith at his task was thirsty work for those who had frequent reason to use his services. Indeed, many a smith was also a beer-seller and publican. Richard Hurst, who died in 1878 at the age of 62, was one of them. He weighed 22 stone and, unusually for the time, was a vegetarian.

There were two distinct types of forgeworker: the blacksmith and the farrier, the latter in theory dealing with horses rather than people. The farrier made and fitted horseshoes and practised horse veterinary work as well. He kept a cupboardful of his own secret remedies, devised from herbs and other vegetable matter and unlikely animal matter (including manure and cobwebs), which he fashioned into potions and lotions, powders and purges, medicine balls, oils and soothing balms for working horses. He could lance an abscess, apply a poultice, file a tooth – and would pull human teeth as well, when asked. Joe Trevinnick of Cornwall, who retired as a fisherman shortly after World War II, claimed that when he was a lad the villagers had better, stronger teeth from eating tougher food, including raw turnips, while the men and boys all chewed tobacco too, which he thought must have helped to preserve their teeth. But if someone did suffer from toothache he went to the smithy and, for sixpence a tooth, the troublesome peg was extracted with a pair of tongs (or a strong finger and thumb) with nothing more than a quick visit to the ale-house to cushion the pain.

The profession of farrier, however, was no longer recorded on the 1891 census. He had been replaced in his role as horse doctor by the newly professional veterinary surgeon for whom he had been making instruments, and sometimes the farrier became a qualified vet himself, or simply a blacksmith. At the same time, the traditional blacksmith increasingly became an agricultural mechanic mending farm machinery, and a bicycle repairer.

George Dew's father was a moderately prosperous village builder, carpenter and blacksmith who had inherited the family firm started by George's great-grandfather during the 18th century. Young Dew was apprenticed as a carpenter on leaving school at 15, no doubt wearing the typical carpenter's square paper hat as he worked knee-deep in sawdust and wood-shavings. At the workbench nearest the little fireplace was a special resting-place for the pot of pitch, heated on the fire before being used to seal coffins – for many carpenters were also coffin-makers and undertakers.

Coffin-making was often a sideline for wheelwrights too, who, with the decrease in demand for horsedrawn vehicles, became more general carpenters. One village wheelwright and undertaker, who died in his eighties before World War I, had been the local bee expert. He used to stand all his straw skeps on offcuts from the thick elm slabs used for making coffins, turning them into solid stools with red-painted cartwheel spokes as legs. This delightful old villager continued the traditional practice of giving a swarm of bees to newly-weds to sweeten their marriage with honey.

Some villages also had a cooper, a man who knew the art of shaping and steaming tongues of wood to form watertight containers for every conceivable purpose from 108-gallon ale butts to the little bever-barrels in which farmworkers took their refreshment into the fields. For the cottage he made wooden water-buckets and milk-pails, wash tubs, pickling vats, flour vats, butter churns, cheese moulds and presses, and a whole range of cheap storage vessels for every type of food and commodity. He also converted old barrels into dog-kennels, bowls and tubs, or cottage chairs complete with rockers.

Although the cooper was vital in larger villages, the introduction of cheap galvanized and enamelled buckets, bowls and pots saw the virtual disappearance of his trade. Between the 1850s and 1890s, the number of village coopers dropped sharply and by the early years of the 20th century they had become rare. Many diversified, as they always had: William Dalley of Bedfordshire, for example, was, in the 1830s, a cooper, ploughwright, carpenter and rat-catcher; and a slightly desperate cooper at Hailsham in East Sussex put up a sign:

As other people have a sign,
I say – just stop and look at mine!
Here, Wratten, cooper, lives and makes
Ox bows, trug-baskets, and hay-rakes.
Sells shovels, both for flour and corn,
And shauls, and makes a good box-churn,
Ladles, dishes, spoons and skimmers,
Trenchers, too, for use at dinners.
I make and mend both tub and cask,
And make 'em strong, to make them last.
Here's butter prints, and butter scales,
And butter boards, and milking pails.
N'on this my friends may safely rest –
In serving them I'll do my best;
Then all that buy, I'll use them well
Because I make my goods to sell . . .

The good Mr Wratten had embraced the work of several other traditional rural craftsmen who worked in wood in their own little workshops, woodland yards and coppices – the men who kept the woods alive with work and purpose, making things for their villages before they made things for the factories. A few of them survived into the 20th century, and a few survive even now, but the local woods close to where I live, once full of such men, are quiet and lonely without them: only one or two still work there, alone.

Iron and wood. There was also earth and stone to be won from the land. George Swinford, born in 1887, came from a long line of stonemasons stretching back at least to his great-grandfather. George began work at the age of 12, leaving home with his father at six in the morning to walk four miles to work. It was a long day working until eight in the evening, with half an hour for breakfast and tea and an hour for dinner, six days a week. In 1902 George walked ten miles on Monday mornings to work on a large new house, lodging in a local cottage for the week and walking home again on Saturday evening, often potting a rabbit on the way with the aid of a catapult. Saturday evening was pay-time for the farmworkers: in summer the wages were paid at eight in the evening in the farmhouse kitchen. Wives and children waited impatiently in the lane to spend the money immediately in the village shop.

Another worker in stone was the millwright, who dressed the big grinding-stones that turned grain into flour. It comes as a surprise, perhaps, that many private village watermills were still actively grinding corn in the 1930s, though many others were already beginning to slow down in the 1850s and many more fell into disuse from the 1880s. Most have long since been converted into private

RIGHT **Two underground Dorset quarriers: Harry Chincher (standing) and Walter Brown.**

dwellings but were once important places, major architectural features in the landscape playing a major role in the local economy and adding to the continual activity and noisiness of the countryside. The miller was not a man to be crossed and in earlier times he was often in close partnership with the lord of the manor, who compelled all the village's grain producers to use the miller's service at a monopoly price. The lord owned the mill, the miller rented it and this was the case right through the working life of most mills. The millhouse was home as well as mill and it usually had its own dairy and assorted farm-buildings for calves, pigs, poultry and other livestock, with stabling for the horses and carts and a few acres of land for grazing – the miller was one of the many local smallholder tenants.

George Elliott, born in 1892, worked as a collar-maker in his little stone terraced cottage in North Newington. Lame from the age of five, as a boy he was apprenticed to a saddler in Moreton-on-the-Marsh before becoming a journeyman for a Banbury harness-maker. He then set himself up in business, mainly making carthorse collars, and during the war he made scores of saddles for export. After the war the business gradually dwindled and he was reduced to making dog-collars, leashes and handbags, but it was boosted again in the 1950s by the opening of a new riding school nearby. Another saddler in Berkshire at that time specialized in making racing saddles at East Ilsley, working with pigskin in what used to be the saddler's shop of a large old estate. The 300-year-old shop had a stone block in the yard where knackered horses were slaughtered and their hides skinned and tanned by the estate saddlers – not a pleasant job, perhaps, but carters were devoted to

An old mill near
Ilfracombe, Devon.

Blacksmiths often worked closely with wheelwrights. At Stratton, Cornwall, the wheelwright's shop stood across the street from the forge and the two trades came together for this photograph in about 1895.

their horses and often missed them so much that when an animal died the saddler might be asked to make up a collar from its hide 'to feel that he still had part of his old horse about the place'.

Most saddlers set up their businesses in market towns rather than villages, but in Eastergate in Sussex Will Walling (known to all the children as 'Uncle Will') was still running a thriving trade after World War II and was remembered affectionately by Barbara Ovstedal who, many years later, could still evoke the smell of the delicious mixture of leather, polish and rope in his shop. 'Uncle Will' made saddles and tack by hand, as he had since his initial apprenticeship at the age of 13 in his father's old shop. He started with waxing the thread ends before progressing to stitching and then began to make horse-collars – up to 50 a season – each carefully tailored to an individual horse so that it fitted comfortably. Later, when the shop was his own, Will would take delight in driving his pony cart around the farms after the harvest to chat with the carters

and take the harness to pieces so that he could give them a thorough scrub and repair them before oiling the leather and painting the wooden parts bright cobalt blue.

Will Walling also sold brushes, currycombs, horse oils and whips, and repaired boots and shoes. In the latter respect he was a cobbler, a trade looked down upon by the real village shoemaker who made rather than repaired. Shoemakers were also called 'snobs' – a word applied to them before being used to describe social climbers. They made shoes to fit the individual foot, but above all they made boots, good tough working boots that took half a day to make and fitted perfectly for nine shillings a pair at the turn of the century, when the work was all still done by hand or with the help of a foot-pedalled contraption. But mass-produced footwear reduced the shoemaker to a cobbler and he deserted the village for the town. However, he lasted a lot longer than many cottage industries which were once the lifeblood of the village.

For much of the Victorian period all these craftsmen were essential to the village. Their skills and products were necessary to the villagers, and the craftsmen and traders were important cogs in the wheels that pumped life into the village. But during the first few decades of the 20th century, the rural crafts became overwhelmed and their practitioners a dying race, remaining only as quaint tourist attractions. The once essential 'village servant' became the servant of richer patrons, rather than to fellow villagers. When their products became superfluous – when villagers began to buy mass-produced essential items instead – then the craftsmen became superfluous. No longer necessary to the village, it no longer mattered if they were not true villagers. They were in limbo, their workshops set apart. The true value of craft lies in being useful and necessary. It has now become an art for 'self-expression' – utility no more. The old village workshop has become a 'studio'.

CHAPTER 6

Cottagers

Cottages characterize a village even more than its church and big houses. Squire, parsons, farmers and worthies were all important and often left lasting evidence in the landscape, but their numbers were tiny and their lives would have been meaningless without the context of cottagers. The great majority of village people, wielding influence precisely because of their majority, were ordinary estate workers, farmworkers, fisherfolk, miners, quarriers, domestic workers, smallholders and cottagers. Their lives were certainly influenced by the village élite but not, perhaps, with such a degree of dominance as we tend to suppose. Even the lord of the manor was merely a background figure to most villagers who simply got on with the business of living, with personal griefs and pleasures that had little to do with squires, vicars or anybody else.

It is difficult for us now to slip inside the skin of a Victorian cottager and really know what village life was like then. And those contemporaries who described the old life were all too often literate observers rather than born-and-bred cottagers, so that we cannot always rely on the images they have bequeathed.

There were substantial regional variations in the life of the cottager, as well as changes in condition over the period as a whole, and a wide range of circumstances within each village, making it impossible to generalize about cottage life. Discount the romantically pretty or romantically abject images painted and photographed by countless Victorians and Edwardians; remember instead that the Victorian villagers had no experience of our own standard of living. This does not mean that they felt any unhappier, or happier, than most of us now. They compared themselves with each other, not with those who lived in a different world whether by social status, by region or by period, and their perspectives were relative.

The large army of landless labourers, without even rented land to work and entirely dependent on the goodwill and changing fortunes of landowners and tenant farmers for their livelihood, were at the very bottom of the pyramid in the agricultural village. It was mainly these workers who lived in the cottages. They did not share proportionately the agricultural prosperity of the early 1870s, and it was

they who deserted the land in their many thousands in a desperate search for better prospects in industry or overseas.

In spite of their general illiteracy and lack of knowledge of much of the world beyond the village, many 19th-century farmworkers were highly skilled. Yet they suffered bottom-of-the-heap wages, very long working hours and bad working and living conditions. Some, however, were better appreciated than others, and most valued of all were those who worked with animals.

A carter or ploughman was in charge of the heavy horses that were the farm's power engines. Big, slow, steady animals, they did virtually everything today's tractors can do and carted anything a man could not carry on his own back about the farm or to the village or station. For about 150 years, throughout the 19th century and halfway through the 20th, the horse was the prime locomotive force on the farm and was a precious beast: a good carter often valued his horses even above his wages, his cottage and his wife.

Carter Trinder, described by Arthur Gibbs as 'one of the cheeriest fellows that ever worked', was the father of 21 children, all by the same wife, but 'he never seemed to be worried in the slightest degree by domestic affairs, and was always happy and healthy and gay'. To support this huge family, Trinder's wages in the 1890s were a mere 12 shillings a week but his sons worked in the fields as well and were virtually self-supporting from the age of ten.

Carters usually received top rates, earning even more than shepherds, who were men of great importance in certain regions and who lived for their sheep and took orders from no master. Although there are many recorded memories of Victorian shepherds, they were essentially private men, loners except when they gathered at the markets and sheep fairs, and they tended to live apart from

OPPOSITE **The Wheeler family, Berkshire, in the late 19th century. Many cottagers were also farmworkers.**

LEFT **A Dorset labourer coming home.**

133

ABOVE **A carter bringing horses back to the yard near Wincanton, Somerset, in 1900.**

ABOVE RIGHT **William Sheppard, a Sussex shepherd, wearing the practical smock or 'round-frock'.**

the villagers, keeping their own counsel. Old Howell of Chesterton, for example, who was 92 in 1872 (and his wife 91), had been a shepherd all his life and would leave home at daybreak, never returning until night, whatever the weather, and during lambing would naturally stay with the flock, taking shelter in his wheeled hut.

There is a touching little tale recalled by a village wheelwright born in the 1820s who, as a small boy, went with his father to take a shepherd's coffin to his widow's cottage. The woman was deeply distressed that her late husband had rarely been to church since their wedding 60

years earlier and might have a little trouble getting through the gates of heaven. She was reassured when the undertaker carefully placed a tuft of sheepswool in the dead man's hand, an ancient custom to show that he was a shepherd, for which his understanding Maker would willingly excuse his absence from church, knowing that a shepherd must always be with his flock.

Those who worked with cows were next in the agricultural hierarchy and, last of all, the general farm-workers, often skilled all-rounders who could be relied upon to help with whatever task was in hand, whether with

Women working at Akeld Farm in Glendale, Northumberland, at the turn of the century. In early Victorian times there were almost as many women involved in farmwork as men.

livestock or crops or maintenance around the farmyard and the fields. Much of their work was laboriously hard and this was their safeguard as well as their burden: farms needed to employ plenty of human labour until mechanized equipment became more widely available and the steam machines, or 'sheenies', came into the fields with their own travelling gangs.

Some women were successful farmers in their own right, and Thomas Hardy wrote graphically about their lives. Others became shepherds or handled cattle – many were milkers and experts in the dairy, making butter and cheese long after later Victorian farmers' wives and daughters had decided that dairywork was beneath them. They handled horses, too, and many could plough as good a furrow as any man. Miss Cowley, of Hardwick, was described by her own sister as a most manly woman who was able to do any job on the farm and was a very good ploughwoman. Unfortunately she fell pregnant when employed as an undercarter: the head carter clearly took her role too literally.

Before World War I farm cottages with a garden were rent-free and extra land could be rented at sixpence a rod. The tied-cottage system developed mainly in the later years of the 19th century to offer farmworkers rent-free homes as long as they worked on the farm, and they were usually accommodated on or near the farms which employed them, rather than in the village. By the end of the 1930s, 97 per cent of farmworkers' homes were tied cottages built by private landowners.

By then the young, it seems, were not prepared to work as hard and as long as the older men. One Sussex labourer in the 1920s said gruffly that when he was young he had worked from four in the morning until sunset, with nothing but a bit of fat pork for breakfast and bread and cheese for dinner; the young, he scoffed, insisted on beef *and* mutton dinners, and pudding, and demanded holidays 'same as if they were gents'.

Diet generally improved in the final quarter of the 19th century with northerners eating better than southerners, largely because of the difference in wage levels. An 1840s Wiltshire labourer's family, for example, existed mainly on bread, potatoes, a little butter and tea, with beer as a luxury and very occasionally a bit of cheese, bacon or fat. In other counties some cottage families of the same period enjoyed a Sunday joint with vegetables and pudding; in Lincolnshire some could afford bacon every day and also adequate milk (not a common part of the rural diet), while in Yorkshire and Northumberland they might have their own house cow and a grain allowance. Twenty years later the regional differences were much the same but white baker's bread had become the staple food, closely followed by homegrown potatoes; meat (including bacon) was still a luxury in the south, but tea and sugar were increasingly important. A national enquiry into the diet of labourers in 1863 revealed that it was better to live in Lancashire (porridge, coffee, meat, rice-pudding, ale, toasted cheese and bacon) than poor old backward Wiltshire (watery broth, cabbage, bread, potatoes, tea, onions and perhaps bacon).

Butcher's meat, especially beef, had been something of a luxury reserved for the working head of the household, until it became cheaper when frozen imports came over from America and Australia in the 1880s. Other cheap imported foods in the late 1870s and early 1880s also benefited the average cottager, adding variety as well as quantity to the diet, and by the 1890s most cottagers in most parts of the country had fresh meat at least once a week and bought delivered town groceries like tinned meat, coffee, dried fruit, jam, cocoa and fish, all of which meant an increasing heap of rubbish – tins and jars and other things.

In country areas, rubbish was disposed of as it always had been: by composting, partial burning, dumping and burial. Most cottagers with a garden or allotment had a compost heap for organic waste, while durables which really were beyond repair or recycling were buried in pits at the end of the garden or in nearby woods. It was not until after World War II that local councils began to collect refuse on a regular fortnightly basis from rural households.

Most organic kitchen waste was fed to the traditional cottage pig, which remained the cottager's major invest-ment in many places throughout Victorian times and beyond. Many families would obtain a young weaner and rear it carefully to provide them with a winter's worth of pork and bacon. Some would go further, breeding from a sow and rearing a litter, and though most could barely afford to fatten one pig, some kept three pigs to cover the cost for their feeding – one for the miller, one to buy more and one to kill for the kitchen. Pig meat was salted down to last for months or smoked as bacon or converted into spiced sausages.

Pigs are lovable animals of considerable character and were often a source of affectionate pride to cottage families. Flora Thompson, author of *Larkrise to Candleford*, remarked: 'Men callers on Sunday afternoons came, not to see the family, but the pig, and would lounge with its owner against the pigsty door for an hour, scratching piggy's back.' But pork and pig fat were more important than pig talk and were often the only meat cottage children were given to eat, so pigs were fed on whatever could be found – kitchen scraps and gleanings until the time came to fatten them with barley a few weeks before the final moment of truth: killing the pig, one of the most important days in the calendar. The pampered pig was given no food the day before, to its agitated disbelief, in preparation for the local pig-killer who would tie the pig, protesting loudly, by a rope around the upper muzzle and quickly pole-axe it before cutting its throat. The blood was collected (for black pudding), the hairs scorched off and the skin scoured in boiling water, then the carcass was suspended by pulley, head down from a beam, to be split and hung for a day before being butchered and jointed ready for salting. No doubt a little piece of liver would be taken discreetly down the lane to a struggling widow.

Some cottagers kept chickens, too, and grazed their geese on commonland or kept a turkey in the shed. Some bred rabbits for meat and pelts; some kept a goat or two tethered on the verges, but the cottager's cow was a rarer beast. Wild birds were caught by some for the table blackbirds, sparrows, pigeons and rooks in particular. Some villages specialized in rearing ducks – the 'miserable' hamlets of Fencott and Murcott on Otmoor, for example, where the land lay so low that it was partially flooded every winter and, when the floods subsided, smelled distinctly

fishy. The ducks, however, loved it, and although their ponds were muddy, the beautiful Aylesbury table birds were always as white as snow. They were destined for Smithfield market, though even just before World War I the locals had done little to set up any supply system. Instead it was organized by Smithfield salesmen; the locals killed and partially plucked the birds, packed them into Smithfield crates and sent them by carrier to Bicester railway station. The carrier and the railway charges were

The essential cottage pig, an important capital investment giving excellent returns in meat for many months, and a source of great pride.

paid by Smithfield and there was still an ample net sum for the smallholders.

In coastal villages cottagers had a choice of work and more chose the sea than the land. Their tasks varied considerably according to the season, the region, the type of catch and local customs. The social structure of fishing villages changed with the century: as sail gave way to steam, syndicates began to take over the fleets so that men who had been skipper-owners became answerable to organizations, while the men who had shared catch profits as crew became wage-earning 'sea labourers'. The foreshore continued to attract cocklers, mussel-rakers and other beach gleaners, while the quayside gave ample opportunity for gossiping as nets were mended and boats repaired. The community embraced a wide range of sea-based trades and callings, from smugglers and salvagers to lifeboat crews and coastguards, and it was a very different world to that of the landbound agricultural village.

✂

Cottagers have always been in need of a supplementary income. As smallholders they converted homegrown produce into saleable articles and processed food for their own use and, when times were hard, exchanged surpluses for whatever they needed, in kind or in cash, relying on their own livestock and crops or scavenging for raw materials. As these incidental trades contributed an increasing proportion of the family's income, and with more and more members of the family helping the woman on her production line, they began to use raw materials bought from outside sources. They became 'workers' more than basic producers, selling their wares at fairs and town markets.

OPPOSITE **Women skaning mussels in the coastal town of Whitby, North Yorkshire.**

The next stage in this production process was the organization of individual efforts by agents who recognized that they could use the cottagers as a cheap workforce and could buy their output at rock-bottom prices, then sell them in bulk for a good profit in towns and cities. Typically, an agent would meet representatives from the village at a central place in town and collect from them the villagers' finished items in exchange for new work-packs of raw materials and a few pence pro rata. Alternatively, cottagers delivered their work to the village shopkeeper (with whom the agent had an arrangement) in exchange for food and other goods.

Some of the cottage industries became established as workshops which continued to serve their own villages rather than agents and towns. They included not just blacksmiths and assorted workers in wood, leather and clay but also those who used canes, osiers and rushes for basketry and chair seats, and those who used hemp for ropes and nets. Hemp workers tended to live in fishing villages, and their trade persisted in some places into the 20th century. One extraordinary rope-making 'village' located inside a Derbyshire cave at Castleton's Peak Cavern only closed completely in 1975. Famous in the 17th century, and a local attraction on every traveller's itinerary, it was described in 1681 by Izaak Walton's friend, Charles Cotton:

Now to the cave we come wherein is found
A new strange thing; a village underground.
Houses and barns for men and beasts behoof
With distant walls under one solid roof
Stacks of hay and turf, which yield a scent . . .

Several rope-making families lived within the cave next to their rope-walks until the smoke from the cottage chimneys made the working atmosphere impossible and they were

demolished. But they kept on with their rope-making, each traditional cavern family with its own rope-walk working six days a week in the 19th century to produce everything from clothes-lines to hangman's ropes, and after dark they made whiplashes by candlelight.

Herbert Marrison was the last of them – he retired at the age of 90 in 1975 when his trade ceded to mass production of synthetic-fibre ropes. Marrison was a traditionalist, spinning his own retted hemp before twisting it into ropes with the help of a system of T-posts, geared wheels and a stone-weighted cart to maintain the correct tension during the rope-making. Most other rope-makers scattered through Derbyshire's villages had ceased trading by the end of the 19th century, save John Barber of Tansley who continued working until the late 1930s in a business which his grandfather had established in 1810.

The major raw material for cottage industries for centuries was wool. Most women and many men knew how to prepare, spin and dye a fleece and specialists evolved for every stage of the complicated process of converting what sheep wore on their backs into something people could wear on theirs. As useful cottage industries, spinning and weaving were killed off after the invention of spinning jennies and the steam-powered looms of the early 19th century. It was not until the 1860s, however, that the wool industry as a whole became largely mechanized and the cottagers' skills became redundant as factories took over their work.

In some parts of the country, cottagers specialized in hand-knitting and in the north of England this continued as an organized industry until the 1870s. Children could attend knitting schools, and cottagers knitted stockings, underwear and jackets for fishermen and a wide range of gloves, stockings, caps and clothes for the general market. When machines began to take over many knitters found themselves relying on the parish poor relief. In most villages hand-knitting died out by the late 19th century, though knitters in the more remote coastal, island and fishing villages continued to produce their strongly regional styles into the present century. In Dorset, hand-knitters continued to make gloves and produced 3000 pairs a week for the armed services during World War II.

Ruddington, in Nottinghamshire, was the largest framework-knitting village south of the Trent by the mid 19th century, and its stockingers worked on handframes based on an invention by a Nottinghamshire clergyman in 1589. Stockingers also thrived in large numbers in Leicestershire: in 1792 about 40 per cent of the county's population was engaged in framework knitting and in 1844 about 21,000 of Britain's 48,000 frames were in Leicestershire. There were still many frames in the county's villages in the 1920s, though by then they were huge and steam-powered.

Home cotton-weaving also suffered a dramatic collapse when handlooms were replaced by power looms. In 1820 there had been 360,000, but ten years later there were only 200,000 handlooms. By the late 1830s some regions which had relied heavily on cottage cotton work were in deep trouble and by 1850 cotton handlooms were rare and the cottage industry was dead.

Lace-making began as a cottage industry in England during the 16th century with the settlement of Flemish lace-makers in Bedfordshire and Buckinghamshire. By the mid 19th century, lace-makers in several counties were delivering their finished work to the village shop in exchange for goods. From there, agents took the lace to sell at the big lace markets in London and other centres. But as a cottage industry lace-making was dying for much of the Victorian age, and was dead before its queen.

Hand-stitching leather and suede gloves was another

eye-bending and painstaking cottage industry and huge numbers of women became cottage glove-makers, working under a master-glover acting as their agent. Early in the 19th century many such women were supporting the whole family during periods of agricultural depression, but as the century progressed, handmade leather and suede gloves had to compete with cheap French imports and machine-made cotton, wool and silk gloves produced in Nottinghamshire and Leicestershire. The cottage industry revived in the 1840s and in some places continued to thrive for the next 60 years as outworkers were employed by the factories. Even in 1926 new cottages were being built for glove-makers around Charlbury and Woodstock in Oxfordshire.

In some regions cottagers became button-makers – silk buttons in Staffordshire, for example, or gold and silver wire buttons. Since the 1620s Dorset had specialized in making buttons from sheep's horn covered with linen, and this cottage industry was at its height in the mid 19th century. But at the Great Exhibition of 1851 a new linen-button machine was displayed and the Dorset cottage industry crashed within three years. It was such a major local disaster that the county's gentry funded mass migrations of almost entire villages to Canada and Australia for those in search of a new life.

Straw-plaiting was another important and widespread cottage industry. The straw was plaited for making into hats and bonnets – the making-up being a separate cottage industry – and it was one of those occupations which involved the whole family as it needed no equipment and you could plait wandering about the village or on your way to work in the fields. The industry declined with the introduction of Chinese imports, after the 1870s, and collapsed when Japanese plait was imported in large quantities during the early 1890s, though it persisted

A straw-plaiter, c. 1916. Straw-plaiting lengths to be made into hats and bonnets was a common cottage industry, especially in arable areas, and was greatly encouraged by parishes wishing to avoid paying out poor relief.

A cottage porch and sink in Devon, 1907.

around the Luton area right up to 1930. Cottage hat-stitchers continued their separate industry by adapting to treadle sewing machines which were still at work in the 1920s and, here and there, into the 1990s too.

These, then, were the main cottage industries though there were countless others scattered around the countryside and special to certain localities. Most had ceased to be significant by 1900 and many had declined almost before Victoria came to the throne – ribbon-weaving in Coventry and wool-combing in Yorkshire, for example, were in trouble in the 1830s, frame-knitters in the East Midlands were declining in the 1850s, coppermines in Cornwall were waning in the 1860s, and leadmining had collapsed by the 1870s. Some of these industries left their mark on the villagescape. Chain, nail and file-makers in the West Midlands had forge-hearths in their cottage gardens; framework knitters and handloom weavers often had purpose-built cottages with long windows, Derbyshire leadminers (usually smallholders) tended to live in scattered longhouses, and whole new villages were built by the collieries in the mid 19th century for self-employed miners who contracted themselves as members of gangs to exploit a particular site and were paid by the amount extracted, be it coal or lead.

Many of these groups were more fortunate in their premises than most cottagers. The typical old cottage had an earthen floor sprinkled with sand and rushes (the proudest housewives would sweep the sand into artistic whorls and patterns), no ceiling under the rafters that supported the tatty thatch, wattle-and-daub or cob-and-straw walls, sewage-saturated surroundings, and all-in-one-room sleeping (often all in one bed, too) which was at the same time both stuffy and cold. Draughts were inescapable and even up to World War I floorboards were unusual downstairs and only gappily spanned the inter-floor beams so that the bedroom (if there was one) had a direct view into the living-room below.

Although new cottages were being built of brick after the removal of the brick tax in 1850, many rural cottagers still lived in their old dwellings made of much cheaper and more transient local materials – no doubt envious of the fired clay tiles or slates that roofed the modern homes, with their partitioned rooms, fitted windows and planked floors. Some 50 years later, when the old queen had died, most of those crumbling old cottages had died too, largely un-mourned by villagers who had largely moved away anyway.

The Northamptonshire poet John Clare (1793–1864) was born in one such tumbledown hovel. The son of a poor labourer, he wrote vividly about the village and farm life of his time. Many other writers and poets have described village life, though rarely from personal experience as cottagers. George Mitchell revealed 'pastoral' life for what it really was for a farm labourer in the 1870s, and Richard Jefferies (1848–87) is an excellent source for the 1880s.

Jefferies was not a cottager but he was a countryman, born in what remains the resolutely rural county of Wiltshire (which he himself described as 'the rudest and most illiterate county of the West') at Coate Farm, near Swindon. A novelist and romantic, and in love with nature, Jefferies was also a journalist, an observer of men and of agriculture as an industry. He was alive to the big social changes in rural areas during his short lifetime, including invasions by suburban day-trippers. He put his finger on the pulse of the countryside in 1877 when he described the 'strange indifference to time which seems to brood over the village. Even at their work in the fields the men and women do not hasten; their arms move slowly, and ever and anon they pause and talk. There is no noise of whirling wheels, no bustle and puff and hurry. The very sun appears to hang in the sky. The days are longer here .... The clock in the church stopped half a generation ago ....'

Jefferies wrote often of cottagers. In *The Toilers of the Field* he describes exactly how so many labourers' cottages were born – not a subject often covered in books. He chooses a squatter, whose first task is to establish his rights to a plot by enclosing it with a low earth bank planted with a hedge of fast-growing elder bushes and interrupted by a stick-gate with a padlock to secure his 'garden'. This is not a fire-in-the-hearth-by-sunset squatter but a methodical man whose home requires months of deliberation and preparation before the first brick or stone can be set. He must find a source of building materials – bricks in clay country, stones from a farm quarry. His employer might let him have most of the stone free and even lend him a horse and cart to carry it from the quarry and will give him building timber, for a nominal price at most.

Next the labourer must find lime for mortar – and there is bound to be at least one local mason working for farmers in the area, mending their walls and putting up pig-stys, who would be willing to spend his Saturday afternoon or weekday evenings helping the potential cottager by doing the actual building, with the cottager acting as hod-bearer and mortar-mixer. Having chosen the site within the garden, usually backing on to a ditch to act as both sewer and cesspool, they set about designing the cottage.

The design is simple: two oblong rooms of similar size on the ground floor, one for living in, with a fireplace and chimney at the end, and the other for sleeping in, with a small shed at one end with an oven in it for baking bread. And that is all. They build the walls up to a little more than head height, put in the roof timbers, thatch with straw or reed – no ceiling beneath the rafters except for a small loft at one end. The walls are whitewashed; the floor is of rammed earth or rough paving stones, the furniture no more than a few stools or chairs (three-legged to sit best on the uneven floor), a cheap table, a couple of shelves and a cupboard. The domestic utensils are a large pot, a saucepan, a few plates and dishes, some knives and spoons, and the mantelpiece is decorated with some cheap china ornaments from the pedlar.

And this was by no means a rude cottage. Even in Jefferies' time, some were built by merely digging four posts into the ground to support crossbeams and the roof, while the walls were wattle sticks daubed with rough mud-plaster mixed with straw or reeds; the roof was single span, the front of the house being higher than the back, and roughly thatched. Or, in contrast, there were squatters who had saved a little money and were good with their hands: they were perhaps thatchers, hedge-layers, tinkers or blacksmiths who had saved maybe £30 and could build quite a good little cottage, ignoring the architects and builders who claimed that such a cottage could not cost less than £120. But the owners of such cottages did the work themselves; they bought cheap second-hand materials and used rough beams to make a two-storey cottage, two up and two at least down, with the essential lean-to shed, whitewashed walls and thatched roof, tidy flagstone floors, perhaps a few prints on the walls (popularly of Dick Turpin on Black Bess) and some good beds upstairs. Sill-green here and there on the roof (as a herb), ivy growing over one end of the house, honeysuckle scrambling over the porch, cabbage roses at the door, and under the windows a profusion of hollyhocks, wallflowers, everlasting sweet peas, columbines and lilies of the valley; thick hedges surrounding the long garden and decorated with wild roses and convolvulus; fruit trees of every kind filling every space and corner (one each of apple, pear, damson, plum, bullace) with an understorey of gooseberry bushes, currants and raspberries; strips of vegetables lining the kitchen garden and a big clump of rhubarb; herbs tucked here and there about the garden – southernwood and mugwort in deference to tradition though rarely actually used, and mint and other pot-herbs; potted geraniums on the window-ledge and, in almost every cottage, a wicker cage over the porch with a captive songbird (usually an 'ousel' – male blackbird), a tame rabbit and a mongrel dog.

If this sounds like the traditional country cottage, well, it was. And, as Jefferies remarked, its picturesque irregularity and home-made feel were far more pleasing than the 'modern glaring red brick and prim slate of dwellings built to order, where everything is cut with a precise uniformity'. The home-made cottage might not have been worth much money (then) but its owner took great pride in his creation and would remain loyal to the place, looking forward to bequeathing it to his children.

Jefferies also described the village farmhouses and tradesmen's houses which had since been divided into two, three or more homes for cottage families. There were also the village cottages which had been built specifically for the labourers, ranging from hovels to proper cottages and modern model cottages, and including in every village at least one cottage which 'carries one's idea of Lilliputian dwellings to the extreme' – converted sheds and outhouses, perhaps one up one down and each room only six feet wide but surprisingly clean, bright, warm and inviting, with the walls literally covered by engravings from the *Illustrated London News*.

Jefferies described a rich cast of cottage characters and

their daily lives in the 1870s: women hastening home from fieldwork at four in the afternoon to prepare the great evening meal taken at half past six or seven, after which the man of the house pottered on his allotment for a while in summer, or perhaps went to the ale-house, then retiring to bed early, since carters had to bait their horses long before dawn the following morning and milkers were at work half an hour later. An early bedtime saved on candles, too.

Cottage women were hospitable people. There was a widespread habit of leaving the doorkey in the lock on the *outside* if a woman was going out for a short while to chat with a neighbour or draw some water. It was a sign that she was out but would be back soon; if she was out all day she would lock the door and remove the key.

In winter, the rain leaked through the thatch of the cottage and seeped in under the door and down the customary steps to dampen the earth or stone floor. Smoke filled the room, stirred by the wind that drove through every gap and defied the draught screens as everybody huddled over the fire for its heat and for its light (saving candles again). 'In the life of the English agricultural labourers,' wrote Jefferies, 'there is absolutely no poetry, no colour. Even their marriages are sober, dull, tame, clumsy and colourless.'

Walter Boniface was a genuine cottager, not a writer, who died in 1940 when he was more than 80 years old, though he was not quite sure how much more. Boniface was able to describe many of the cottages which had long since disappeared in his hamlet, including the small-holding in the Hollow whose ruined walls were still visible in 1900 and the outline of its shed in a clump of hollies, while its old garden was betrayed by fruit trees, gooseberry bushes and snowdrops. The holding had been worked by a couple with a son and daughter who 'got their living quite easily with two cows and some poultry'. The smallholder

The interior of a Shropshire cottage at Lightmoor.

told Walter that, as a small boy, he had been sitting on his father's knee when the man was arrested in the cottage, accused of murdering an excise man who had interfered with his smuggling, a popular local occupation at the time. The hamlet boasted the last illicit still in the county, run by Butner Brown and his large family in a building they called 'The Bolting'.

Walter's father once dug up a small keg of spirits nearby but some one else pinched it while he was finding a barrow to transport it. The death of Butner Brown in the 1850s was remembered by old Mrs Knight, who used to keep a village shop in her outhouse. That shop was not a

Cagebirds (native songbirds) were a popular cottage-door feature.

financial success – Mrs Knight was generous with credit and hopeless with keeping accounts, and eventually she put up a sign:

People came and I did trust them;
I lost my money and their custom.
To lose them both did grieve me sore
So I resolved to trust no more;
And now I sell the best of goods
For money paid me when it should.

Nellie Kewell was born in 1894 in one of a group of cottages known as 'The Barracks' (a name often given to old pauper-houses), though the family soon moved across the green to a larger cottage, where several of her sisters were born. Most people worked for the big estate, including her father who was a painter and decorator: Nellie used to hold up the candles for him as he applied wallpaper. At home the family used water from the well, oil-lamps for lighting, and a copper for laundry – a major weekly task which involved drawing the well water and then heating it on the fire and filling the cottage with steam. There was a wood-fired brick oven for the weekly baking. As tenant of Blossom Cottage, her father took on the traditional job of winding the school clock in its tower each week, climbing up inside the tower on a ladder. The clock was visible all over the valley until the copper-roofed tower was removed during World War II because, they said, Germans might use it as a landmark, but in reality because it had become structurally unsound.

Nellie's nephew, Les Vale, lived with his family in the other half of Blossom Cottage. His father was a baker and confectioner who, as a young apprentice, used to take the farm's horse and cart to deliver bread from about four in the morning, all round the district, and often called at old

Mrs Luff on the hill, who made such excellent and potent country wines.

When Les was six, the growing family moved to an ancient farmhouse up the lane. There were ten children by then, and there never seemed to be enough to eat, though they were all experts at foraging for chestnuts and other

A cottager reading by the fireside in Devon, 1907.

A New Forest gypsy. By the 1870s, the majority of gypsies had become cottage-dwellers.

they never found the smugglers' tunnel said to run from the big house right up to the old chapel and graveyard on the hilltop, where the ghosts of smugglers and highwaymen crossed the road at midnight. But they counted the 72 steps set in the wooded hillside, where three or four centuries ago hooded monks had quietly puffed their way to worship.

Emily Lawrence was born in a smuggler's cottage and has many a tale to tell of how local villagers and farmers would make sure that horses were left grazing in their fields at night to give the smugglers a fresh mount. In the morning a strange horse would be in the field instead, and in exchange a little gift left close by. Emily's mother was also born in the cottage that snuggled rather secretly down a long track which had once been a busier lane between the villages but is now little more than a bridleway. Water was collected from a well in the garden and the family had a smallholding with a few cows, pigs and chickens and some prolific walnut trees.

The cottage seems to have been the home at one time or another of several villagers – Sid Bridger's grandfather lived there, and all the Quinnell brothers who became stonemasons and coppice craftsmen. Emily remembers the chestnut coppices being trimmed out every three years for walking sticks and palings, and George and Dick Quinnell still work in the coppices today, setting up their camps in quiet, isolated patches of woodland whence the gently rising smoke of their bonfires and the steady clop and rasp of their cleaving and peeling betray their whereabouts. Their work is still much the same as it would have been a century and a half ago.

Emily walked through the woods and fields to the little school, as her mother, uncles and aunts had done. Up some steps set in the lane's bank, it was also a sweet-shop and post office, but it closed down as a school when Emily was 11, as there were only a dozen children on its register. Like most

wild food. Their new home had a well 60 feet deep and mother, when drawing the water, was so fearful of losing one of her brood down it that she would line the whole family up against the wall first, giving the front child the task of ensuring that nobody fell in. Otherwise the children had ample freedom to explore the countryside, though other village girls, Emily went into domestic service as soon as she left school, but later worked for many years in the village shop.

As the wealth and involvement of landowners and squires rapidly declined during the early 20th century, under the burden of taxes and estate duty, so too did their traditional building of new rural homes. Increasingly the role of housing shifted on to local government. The first council homes in England were built in the fading years of the 19th century and, while they offered much higher living standards, right from the start planners failed to understand the traditional village. The new homes were built in phalanxes, all together on one site and identical to each other. They were built of brick and concrete, regardless of local materials; they were set back from the street rather than forming part of its frontage; and they paid no heed to vernacular styles but gave a strong impression of having been transplanted from a suburban environment. Instead of being scattered individually so that they could be absorbed into the old village like darns and patches in a well-loved garment, the council houses had laid the ground for building in self-contained bunches which would inevitably create social as well as physical divisions within the village.

Even in the late 1930s a lot of rural people, especially farmworkers, were living in old cottages in need of renovation. Very small and cramped, most had nothing more than a fair-sized living-room and kitchen combined, and seldom more than two bedrooms, if that. Occasionally there might be a small scullery area, and rarely a tiny parlour. The 'bathroom' was a portable tub in the kitchen

handfilled with water heated up on the range. There might be the convenience of a cold-water pump at the back door and almost invariably the inconvenience of an earth closet down the garden. Such cottages were traditionally the homes of large families – half a dozen children crammed into them along with their parents. Almost unanimously,

The interior of the Luff family's home in Sussex in the 1920s.

the farmworkers made it clear that they wanted modern homes, not old cottages.

Townsfolk with romantic ideas were already becoming country weekenders, busily buying up and 'doing up' old cottages within and around villages, letting them stand empty for most of the year and removing them from the pool of village housing, depriving villagers of choice. In addition, the years between the wars saw an influx of 'leisured people and footloose intellectuals' such as artists and writers who fled to the countryside and bought up cottages as permanent homes, taking the cream of what was available so that, again, the low-paid villager lost out. The changing village shape was altering villagers' lives.

On top of everything else, the 1930s were to see a great increase in the proportion of retired people able to rent or buy their own cottage rather than live with relatives or in institutions, as they often had in the past. It was during this period too that short-sighted planners built bungalows for old people on the outskirts of the villages, away from the everyday life of the street, creating a system of segregation, boredom, loneliness and dependence.

Meanwhile, families were becoming smaller but there was an increase in the number of family units, each reasonably requiring its own separate home. By 1939 there was already a housing shortage in rural areas and overall standards were unacceptably low in most villages. At least the new council housing, where available, had the merit of offering a good-size kitchen/living-room with a scullery, wash-house, outbuildings, fuelstores and probably a downstairs parlour, in addition to three good-sized bedroom and an upstairs bathroom – in striking contrast to the cramped, two-up-one-down cottage that the great majority of rural working families lived in.

RIGHT **Maud Bridger's childhood home in the 1920s.**

In 1923, 12-year-old Maud Bridger lived with her grandparents in half a cottage which they rented for 15 shillings a week – a lot of money in those days. This, however, included shooting and fishing rights and use of the fields, on which the family ran a small poultry enterprise. The little cottage had a very old scullery with a copper in it and a funny little sink, a big living-room and, up the rickety stairs, two bedrooms and a landing. The outdoor toilet was 'a bucket under the yew tree'.

The garden was huge, with a big shed, and the Bridgers kept a pig and its litter, four or five goats and some dogs. It was young Maud's job to stump out the goats in the copse before she went to school in the morning and to bring them in again after school and milk them. The family was self-supporting and grandmother took the eggs to town twice a week in the days when there was still a weekly cattle-market there. She and Maud travelled in Potter's old bus and often helped to push it up the hills.

They also sold rabbits, dressed chickens, flowers, and honey from their own hives. Maud collected the eggs from wherever the poultry and ducks had decided to deposit them, and put them into the family's incubators for hatching. She kept a special incubator in her bedroom for a hundred goose eggs, which she turned by hand like a good little fostermother.

At school Maud learned the three Rs and sewing, knitting, history, geography and science. Like everybody else, she left at the age of 14. She wanted to be a dressmaker but found herself working in the kitchens of the big house, where there were ten staff – butler, footman, hallboy, three house and three kitchen maids, and cook-housekeeper – to look after the Colonel, his four daughters and Mademoiselle, known as Selly.

The staff lived on the top floors of the house and were not allowed to speak to the family unless spoken to, which

Maud resented. They had to be formal to the other staff too – Maud, for example, had to call Irene, the lady's maid, 'Miss Button'. She thoroughly disliked the cook-housekeeper, who considered herself to be very grand, and on the day of a big shoot Maud got the giggles when the woman swept in, all airs and graces, in her long white dress and with her hair pinned up, sailing snootily past the assembled gamekeepers.

Maud met her husband, Sid, in 1927, though she had seen him about the village since she was 14 and he a very grown-up 19 or 20. Sid's family had lived in the area since 1600, originally as yeoman farmers. His recent ancestors had been vergers and parish clerks, and the burial register for 26 September 1902 noted: 'William Bridger, Lynch (Woodman's Green), aged 89. Parish Clerk for 52 years, succeeding his father who had the same office from 1818 till 1850' – nearly a century shared between them. John Bridger was churchwarden in 1717 and 1723, so was Nicklas Bridger in 1728. The family had owned a fair amount of property, *and* their own carriage and pair, and old Mrs Bridger used to ride a white horse when she collected the rents.

Sid worked on the roads as foreman for the council and Maud met him when they were working on a new bridge over the valley's stream. She was 16 then and remembered that 'they already used that liquid tar you roll on with gravel on top for some of the roads'. The village children were sent by their mothers to breathe in the hot, tarry fumes from the crossroads' tar-pot fires as it was believed to be good for the chest. Most of the lanes, however, were deep-rutted cart-tracks and stone, and when Maud was 12, old Mr Stubbington was still sitting at the crossroads breaking up big piles of stones tipped there by wagons.

Sid used to leave the house at 5 am in summer to light the tar-pot fire, returning home at about eight in the evening. He would go as far as Halfway Bridge towards Petworth, and out to Harting and Rogate, by bike at first, though later a lorry would pick him up. Few people had cars – the baker and the butcher but otherwise just the gentry, 'except that my grandfather had one when I was 16,' recalls Maud, 'a Renault touring car which did 60 mph on the A3! He was like that. Sid had a motorbike but usually we used pedal bikes.'

Sid volunteered in 1939. The council wanted some men to go out and build an airfield in France and he went at the beginning of 1940. He came home through the beaches at Dunkirk and on D-Day plus 3 he went back with the Royal Engineers to clear mines – crawling on his belly, prodding the ground in front of him with a bayonet and seeing some of his mates blown up. Sid managed to survive and was demobbed in October 1945.

❧

Jessie Booker was born before the century turned. She, too, is known as Maud but was called Jessie at school as that was her first name and was the one they used on the register. There were 11 of them at home – quite a squeeze – though by the time she was 80 Jessie lived alone in that same semi-detached cottage built of bricks made in the brickyard alongside, where her family had worked.

Jessie's father had joined the brickyard at the age of 17 and worked there for 56 years. By the time he became foreman, there were three others working with him, including his brother and brother-in-law, and his sons were gradually taken into the business as well. They all went off to war in 1914 and the yard closed down until they came home again. Four of Jessie's brothers worked with her father at the yard until it finally closed in 1937.

During World War I Jessie went to Portsmouth to cook for the Navy and in due course became, in her own words, a 'chef' in a hotel on the Sussex coast. She never married but came back to her valley to care for the garden her family had tended for so many years, and to care for her ageing family, too. They all seemed to come home again when they were ill or dying, and Jessie would look after them, sleeping on the floor at their bedside when necessary. She is a remarkable woman: until very recently, though in her nineties, she still walked several miles every day to other villages, uphill most of the way, marching resolutely along the middle of the lanes and so deaf that she was quite oblivious of the cars behind her. But she led a charmed life; she said that God always walked beside her along the road, having a chat. Nor was she ever alone in the cottage: she would hear the voices of her parents, especially her mother, almost as if they were with her in the room. Her family has been in the valley 'for ever', its name recorded locally in Elizabethan times, and it persists in the valley today even though Jessie, after a severe stroke, is now living in an old people's home where she is quietly fading away.

The original villagers – those who were born and raised there – are rare now and with their passing the memory of the working everyday village will be lost. Before it is too late, go to the old villagers and listen to them: the village's living past deserves to have its voice heard. We sometimes forget that a village is its *people*, living, breathing, needing to grow and to change. Let them. Let the village itself remain alive – alive with work, alive with energy, alive with the village's own young in homes they can afford. The urbanization of the village has almost succeeded in wiping out the original villager. How dare we!

Glossary of Terms

Aloes   Bitter purgative from aloe leaves.

Band of Hope   Popular 'sobriety and temperance' organization for young people pledged to lifelong abstinence. First formed in the 1840s and 1850s.

Cachous   Breath-sweeteners, usually made from extract of liquorice.

Demesne   A manor house with its adjacent lands which are not let to tenants.

Dwile-flonking   A rough game in which the *dwile* (inflated pig's bladder) is hit with the *flonk* (a flat board).

Glebeland   Land attached to a parish church, originally areas of farmland and woodland set aside by the local lord and held freehold by the priest, who worked it for his own subsistence but who later let it out to tenants as a source of income.

Glee   Glee-singing is unaccompanied part-singing, that is, harmonies (something like a barbershop quartet), a popular leisure pastime often taken very seriously.

Goose-crammers   People who rear and fatten geese.

Grips   Little channels cut into verges to take water away from road and into ditch.

Hiera-picra   Purgative drug from aloes and canella bark.

Hornbooks   'Primers' for children learning to read, with single pages protected by a sheet of very thin, translucent horn.

Inspector of Nuisances   A post involving the inspection of, for example, drains and privies and other potential public nuisances on behalf of the district sanitary authority. For his work as Inspector of Nuisances, George Dew received a salary of £5 a year.

Jalap (or jalop)   A purgative root (ipomoea) from Latin America.

Nuncheon firkin   A barrel of ale or cider taken into the field for light midday refreshment (*nuncheon* means 'noon drink').

Pleach fence   Fence of flexible hazel rods or withies wound basket-fashion between uprights driven into the ground; or a 'living fence', that is, a laid hedge, similarly woven.

Pot-hooks   Hooked handwritten strokes like g, j, y, etc.

Retted   Soaked to soften or rot.

Rod   Unit of area equivalent to a square pole, that is, $5\frac{1}{2}$ yards by $5\frac{1}{2}$ yards.

Skeps   Beehives woven like straw baskets.

Slate club   A local group which had two principal functions: as a sort of informal insurance policy, whose members contributed weekly to a central fund for benefits against misfortune, or acting as a sort of savings club towards Christmas cheer with a Christmas share-out and feast.

Stump out   Stake out, that is, setting a stake for tethering livestock.

Toc H   Signaller's code for the letters T and H, standing for Talbot House (in Poperinghe, France) where the first meeting was held of a society whose aim was to hand on the Great War spirit of comradeship.

Glossary of Writers

Gibbs, J. Arthur (1868–99)   Literary scholar, lover of outdoor life, naturalist and sportsman. The son of a squire, Gibbs wrote about his home village of Ablington, Gloucestershire, in *A Cotswold Village, Or, Country Life and Pursuits in Gloucestershire*.

Grace, Theresa   Spent her early 1920s childhood in a Hampshire downland village which she described in an article in *Countryman* (Summer 1984).

Hughes, Thomas (1822–96)   Born in Uffingham, Berkshire. Novelist (author of *Tom Brown's Schooldays*), judge and Liberal MP. Wrote *The Scouring of the White Horse*.

Jefferies, John Richard (1848–87)   Born at Coates Farm near Swindon, Wiltshire. Naturalist, novelist and journalist, Jefferies wrote many articles and books on country life, notably *The Gamekeeper at Home*.

Jekyll, Gertrude (1843–1932)   Painter, embroiderer and landscape gardener. Created over 200 gardens, many in co-operation with the architect Sir Edwin Lutyens. Wrote many articles and several books, especially about country homes, gardens, cottages and old English household life.

Jones, Sydney R.   Author, artist and architect, with a particular interest in villages and farmsteads, Jones also wrote – and illustrated – touring guides and works on social issues. He often collaborated with Gertrude Jekyll on books about cottages.

Pulbrook, Ernest C.   Author of works on early 20th-century English countryside and rural work.

Trollope, Joanna   Novelist (author of *A Village Affair*) born in a Cotswolds rectory, grand-daughter of a Gloucestershire parson, related to Anthony Trollope.

Vancouver, Charles   Compiled a series of county surveys (Devon, Essex and Cambridgeshire) for the Board of Agriculture and Internal Improvement in the late 18th and early 19th centuries. His *General View of the Agriculture of the County of Devon, With Observations on the Means of Improvement*, was published in 1808.

Young, Rev. Arthur   Clergyman, who wrote a report for the Board of Agriculture (published in 1813) on his native Sussex during the 1790s and early 1800s. Not to be confused with the English agricultural writer and editor Arthur Young (1741–1820), Secretary to the Board and author of several English farming *Tours*.

Bibliography

Addison, William, *English Fairs and Markets* (Batsford, 1953).

Bailey, Brian, *The English Village Green* (Robert Hale, 1985).

Bailey, Jocelyn, *The Village Wheelwright* (Shire, 1975).

Barley, M.W., *The English Farmhouse and Cottage* (Routledge & Kegan Paul, 1961).

Beacham, Peter (ed.), *Devon Building: An Introduction to Local Traditions* (Devon Books, 1990).

Beckett, Arthur, *The Spirit of the Downs* (Methuen, 1909).

Bennett, W.S., *Life on the English Manor* (1937).

Beresford, Maurice, *The Lost Villages of England* (Lutterworth, 1954).

Blum, Jerome (ed.), *Our Forgotten Past* (Thames & Hudson, 1982).

Blunden, Edmund, *English Villages* (William Collins, 1942).

Blythe, Ronald, *Akenfield* (Penguin, 1969).

Bonham-Carter, Victor, *The English Village* (Penguin, 1951).

Briggs, Asa, *A Social History of England* (Pelican, 1987).

Brill, Edith, *Cotswold Crafts* (Batsford, 1977).

Brown, Jonathan, and Ward, Sadie, *The Village Shop* (RDS/Cameron & Hollis/David & Charles, 1990).

Brunskill, R.W., *Traditional Buildings of Britain* (Gollancz, 1985).

Buchan, Ursula, *The Village Show* (Pavilion, 1990).

Budd, Mavis, *Dust to Dust* (J.M. Dent, 1966).

Campbell-Kease, John, *A Companion to Local History Research* (Alphabooks, 1989).

Chapman, Brigid, *West Sussex Inns* (Countryside Books, 1988).

Cobbett, William, *Cottage Economy* (1823; reprint Landsman's Bookshop, 1974).

Cobbett, William, *Rural Rides* (1853).

Cripps, Sir John, *Christmas Coals to Community Care – The countryside, past, present and future* (NCVO, 1984).

Critchley, T.A., *A History of Police in England and Wales* (Constable, 1967).

Daunton, M.J., *Royal Mail, The Post Office since 1840* (Athlone Press, 1985).

Davis, Thomas, *General View of the Agriculture of Wiltshire* (1811).

Ditchfield, P.H., *Old Village Life* (Methuen, 1920).

Eglon Shaw, Bill, *Frank Meadow Sutcliffe, A Selection of His Work* (The Sutcliffe Gallery, 1974).

Filbee, Marjorie, *Cottage Industries* (David & Charles, 1982).

Foster, Janet, and Sheppard, Julia, *British Archives: A Guide to Archive Resources in the United Kingdom* (Macmillan, 1982).

Fowler, J.K., *Records of Old Times* (1891).

French, Mary, *A Victorian Village, A Record of the Parish of Quethiock in Cornwall* (Glasney Press, 1977).

Fussell, G.E. and K.R., *The English Countryman* (Andrew Melrose, 1955).

Fussell, G.E. and K.R., *The English Countrywoman* (Andrew Melrose, 1953).

Fussell, G.E., *The English Rural Labourer* (Batchworth Press, 1949).

Garne, Richard, *Cotswold Yeomen and Sheep* (Regency Press, 1984).

Gibbs, J. Arthur *A Cotswold Village* (Jonathan Cape, 1898).

Godfrey, John, Leslie, Kim, and Zeuner, Diana, *A Very Special County, West Sussex County Council, The First 100 Years* (WSCC, 1988).

Goodenough, Simon, *The Country Parson* (David & Charles, 1983).

Hadfield, John (ed,), *The Shell Book of English Villages* (Michael Joseph, 1980).

Hammond, J.L. and B., *The Village Labourer* (Longmans, Green & Co., 1911).

Hanson, Neil, *Classic Country Pubs, A CAMRA guide* (Pavilion/Michael Joseph, 1989).

Hartley, Dorothy, *The Land of England* (Macdonald, 1979).

Harvey, John H., *Sources for the History of Houses* (British Records Association, 1974).

Hibbs, John, *The Country Bus* (David & Charles, 1986).

Horn, Pamela (ed.), *Oxfordshire Village Life: The Diaries of George James Dew, Relieving Officer* (Beacon, 1983).

Hoskins, W.G., *Local History in England* (Longman, 1972).

Bibliography

Iredale, David, *Discovering Local History* (Shire, 1973).

Jackson, W.A., *The Victorian Chemist and Druggist* (Shire, 1981).

Jeffries, Richard, *The Life of the Fields* (Longmans, Green & Co., 1884). [Also Lutterworth, 1947, and OUP, 1983.]

Jeffries, Richard, *The Toilers of the Fields* (Longmans, Green & Co., 1892).

Jekyll, Gertrude, *Old West Surrey* (Longmans, Green & Co., 1904).

Jones, Sydney, R., *English Village Homes* (Batsford, 1936).

Keith-Lucas, Bryan, *A History of Local Government in the Twentieth Century* (George Allen & Unwin, 1978).

Kilby, K., *The Village Cooper* (Shire, 1977).

Lansdell, Avril, *Occupational Costume* (Shire, 1977).

Lewis, June, R., *The Village School* (Robert Hale, 1989).

Marshall, William, *Review and Abstract of the County Reports of the Board of Agriculture* (1818). [Reprinted David & Charles, 1969].

Marshman, Michael, *The Wiltshire Village Book* (Countryside Books, 1987).

Martelli, George, *The Elveden Enterprise* (Faber, 1952).

Mason, Joy, *Chobham Village Hall 1888–1988* (1988).

Middleton, C.H., *Village Memories* (Cassell & Co., 1941).

Mingay, G.E. (ed.), *The Victorian Countryside* (Routledge & Kegan Paul, 1981).

Mitford, Mary Russell, *Our Village* (Sidgwick & Jackson, 1986).

Muir, Richard, *The English Village* (Thames & Hudson, 1980).

Muir, Richard, *The Lost Villages of Britain* (Michael Joseph, 1982).

Munns, R.T., *Milk Churns to Merry-go-rounds, A Century of Train Operations* (David & Charles, 1986).

Murdoch, Ian, *A Ten Year Diary for Countryfolk 1991–2000* (Self-Publishing Association, 1990).

Nair, Gwyneth, *Highley, The Development of a Community 1550–1880* (Basil Blackwell, 1988).

Newby, Howard, *Country Life, A Social History of Rural England* (Weidenfeld & Nicolson, 1987).

Newby, Howard, *The Countryside in Question* (Hutchinson/HTV, 1988).

Olivier, Edith, *Wiltshire* (Robert Hale, 1951).

Pakington, Humphrey, *English Villages and Hamlets* (Batsford, 1934).

Payne, Shaun, Pailthorpe, Richard, and Beningfield, Gordon, *Barclay Wills' The Downland Shepherds* (Alan Sutton, 1989).

Pingriff, G.N., *Leicestershire* (Cambridge University Press, 1920).

Pitt, W., *General View of the Agriculture of the County of Worcestershire* (1813). [Reprinted David & Charles, 1969].

Pulbrook, Ernest C., *English Country Life and Work* (Batsford, 1922).

Randall, H.J., *History in the Open Air* (George Allen & Unwin, 1936).

Seager, Elizabeth (ed.), *The Countryman Book of Village Trades and Crafts* (David & Charles, 1978).

Smith, David Norman, *The Railway and its Passengers, A Social History* (David & Charles, 1988).

Stenton, Doris M., *English Society in the Early Middle Ages* (Pelican, 1951).

Stephens, W.B., *Sources for English Local History* (Cambridge University Press, 1981).

Tate, W.E., *The Parish Chest* (Phillimore, 3rd ed. 1983).

Thomas, F.G., *The Changing Village* (Thos. Nelson & Sons, 1939).

Tilley, M.F., *Housing the Country Worker* (Faber & Faber, 1947).

Trevelyan, G.M., *English Social History* (Longmans, Green & Co., 1945).

Twinch, Carol, *Women on the Land* (Lutterworth, 1990).

Vancouver, Charles, *General View of the Agriculture of the County of Devon* (1808). [Reprinted David & Charles, 1969].

Webb, S. and B., *English Local Government* (10 volumes – Longmans, Green & Co., 1906–29).

Weir, Christopher, *Village and Town Bands* (Shire, 1981).

West, John, *Village Records* (Phillimore, 1982).

Winchester, Angus, *Discovering Parish Boundaries* (Shire, 1990).

Young, Rev. Arthur, *General View of the Agriculture of the County of Sussex* (1813), also *Hertfordshire* (1804), *Lincolnshire* (1813).

Various articles published over the years in *The Countryman* and in the *Journal* of the Society of Local Council Clerks.

Index

Index

Acknowledgements

The author would like to thank the staff at MERL and WSRO for their efficient and enthusiastic help with picture research, and above all the villagers of Grittleton and Milland for their photographs, their friendship and their memories, most generously shared.

The photographs in *English Villagers* are reproduced by kind permission of the following organizations and individuals who allowed copies to be made from original photographs or supplied prints:

Maud Bridger p. 151

Mary Evans Picture Library pp. 72, front cover (photograph hand tinted by Trevor Lawrence)

Mary Evans Picture Library/Bruce Castle Museum p. 17 (top left)

The Garland Collection, West Sussex Record Office pp. 9, 11, 13, 29, 54, 55, 56, 58, 61, 62 (right), 82, 83, 87, 97, 100, 103 (left), 104, 106, 110, 112 (bottom right), 113, 114, 120 (right), 124, 134 (right), 149

The Sutcliffe Gallery, Whitby pp. 3 (repeated on p. 44), 15, 24, 38 (left), 120, 139, back cover

University of Reading, Institute of Agricultural History and Museum of English Rural Life pp. 6, 16, 18, 21, 26, 28, 30, 31, 32, 34, 36 (left & right), 37, 39, 40, 45, 47, 52, 59, 60, 63, 65, 71, 75, 78, 79, 80, 85, 88, 90, 92, 95, 99, 101, 103 (right), 105, 107, 108, 111, 112 (top left), 115, 117, 118, 121 (left), 122, 123, 125, 126, 129, 130, 134 (left), 135, 137, 141, 142, 145, 146, 147, 148

University of Reading, Institute of Agricultural History and Museum of English Rural Life/Dorset County Museum, Dorchester pp. 22, 35, 38 (right), 41, 50, 86, 116, 128, 133

University of Reading, Institute of Agricultural History and Museum of English Rural Life/Mrs Iris Moon (Wilder Photographs) pp. 49, 62 (left), 67, 68, 70, 132

The remaining photographs were supplied by the author.